The Chocolate Cake Sutra

The Chocolate Cake Sutra

INGREDIENTS FOR A SWEET LIFE

GERI LARKIN

HarperSanFrancisco
A Division of HarperCollins*Publishers*

Acknowledgments are gratefully made to reprint an excerpt from "Easter Coker" from *Four Quartets*, copyright © 1940 by T. S. Elliot and renewed 1968 by Esme Valerie Eliot, reprinted by permission of Harcourt, Inc.; and to Willaim J. Higginson, for the translation of the haiku by Bashô ("old pond"), from *The Haiku Handbook: How to Write, Share, and Teach Haiku*, published by Kodansha International, copyright © 1985 by William J. Higginson. Used by permission of the translator.

HarperCollins books may be purchased for educational, business, or sales promotional use. For information please write: Special Markets Department, HarperCollins Publishers, 10 East 53rd Street, New York, NY 10022.

HarperCollins Web site: http://www.harpercollins.com

HarperCollins®, 🏭®, and HarperSanFrancisco™ are trademarks of HarperCollins Publishers.

FIRST EDITION

Library of Congress Cataloging-in-Publication Data

Larkin, Geraldine, A.
The chocolate cake sutra : ingredients for a sweet life / Geri Larkin. — 1st ed.
p. cm.
ISBN: 978-0-06-083695-5
ISBN-10: 0-06-083695-4
1. Success—Religious aspects. 2. Conduct of life. 3. Spiritual life. I. Title.
BL65.S84L37   2006
294.3'444—dc22   2006043503

07 08 09 10 11 RRD(H) 10 9 8 7 6 5 4 3 2 1

This book is dedicated to my mother, for her courage.

Praise be, my Lord, for our sister,

Mother Earth,

Who sustains and governs us

And brings forth diverse fruits with

Many-hued flowers and grass.

—St. Francis of Assisi

Contents

Thank-yous:

To Andrea Pedolsky for hanging in there for this book before moving into the world of salaries. I will miss you desperately. To the HarperSanFrancisco team for being the bodhisattvas of the publishing world. I bow, in particular, to Eric Brandt for his ability to give me clear and upright feedback and to Renee Sedliar, who was the first Harper editor to believe in me. Renee, you are Tara incarnate. To my sangha family, especially Koho Vince Anila and Brahana Sarah Addae Pizzimenti, who made it possible for me to leave Still Point with a happy heart. To my dear and loyal friends, especially Joy Naylor and David Horowitz: I think this might be the first Buddhist-oriented book I've written that doesn't have stories in it about either of you. To Jill Collman for the best chocolate cake recipe ever. To Sarth and Jamie for picking me to be the mom. To Patty for choosing Sarth to be her dad; and to Neptune the cat for teaching me how to live my life. I am grateful every day.

Note to My Readers

This is not a recipe book, although there is an excellent chocolate cake recipe on page 183. Also I am not advocating chocolate cake for breakfast, although it has been my breakfast of choice for the last twenty years. I just substitute soy flour to make it legal.

Prologue

Once upon a time there was a young man named Eugene who was desperate to find a truly holy person with whom he could study. One day as he was gathering wood in the forest, he spied an old man walking calmly down a mountain path. His walk was soft and steady, his half-smile certain. Eugene ran up to him.

"I'm looking for a spiritual teacher. Can you help? Studying alone on this mountain is too hard for me. I get distracted and keep wanting to do things that aren't good for me. Too much television. Double lattes every day. Not enough willpower to turn off my cell phone when it is time to pray. I'm afraid I'll lose the understanding that has come to me after seven years of hard spiritual work if I don't get some regular instruction."

The old man looked at Eugene and replied, "There is a great shaman, a woman named Jaya. It is said that her students awaken quickly, in less than five years. She will only accept students who arrive on foot, so you must walk to her complex. It is three hundred miles from here. I can give you a map."

Figuring that he had nothing to lose, Eugene started walking. What he expected to take three months took three years. The mountains were steep and the weather unkind. He walked through pouring rain, a tornado, three hurricanes, and the biggest snowfall of the last hundred and eight years. Sometimes only the kindness of strangers kept him going—an extra pair of mittens here, a scarf there, hot soup in a thermos.

By the end of the three-year period, Eugene was healthy, strong, and happy. He could feel the earth hold him up and understood the language of most of the birds and animals (with the exception of hummingbirds, who refused to slow down for him ever). In fact, he was so okay that he was tempted to turn around and head back. But he had come far, and curiosity made him want to continue his quest.

At the gate to Jaya's complex, two attendants greeted Eugene. They instructed him to wait in the shrine room until Jaya was ready to meet with him. They told him it shouldn't take long.

Eugene waited and waited. After twelve hours he knocked on the door of the room. A young acolyte was sitting in the hallway guarding the door.

"I need to go to the bathroom."

"You have to stay in the shrine room."

He waited another two hours. Now Eugene really had to go. He knocked again. This time two acolytes were standing in the hall.

"I have to go to the bathroom."

"Just wait."

Another hour passed.

Finally Eugene aimed himself at a corner of the shrine room and peed all over it. Hearing him, the two acolytes rushed in, grabbed him by the shoulders, picked him right off the floor, and started hauling him away.

"How dare you!" shouted the bigger of the two. "This is a holy room!"

Eugene looked at him.

"You show me a place that isn't holy, and I'll pee there!"

"He stays."

It was Jaya.

The Chocolate Cake Sutra

Ode to a Hollywood Crush

The person with a new idea is a crank until the idea succeeds.

—Mark Twain

My Hollywood crush is the reason for this book. Through no fault of my own, I don't watch much television. This means that if I walk into a room and a television happens to be on, I become a deer in headlights, frozen in place, eyes locked onto the screen. Usually this lasts until someone asks me to please move so they can see the screen too. If nobody is in the room I have been known to stand still staring at whatever is on for hours at a time.

The last time I got caught was during an interview with my crush—a rugged, swaggering, digeridoo of a man if there ever was one. He has been my personal bad boy for over twenty years, with his hero roles, eyes to die for, and a grin that can make me forget the unpaid bills that double their amounts whenever I look away.

My crush.

The interview was about a movie he had just directed. It was about Jesus Christ. As a card-carrying Buddhist, I have always been moved to tears by the last hours of the life of Jesus. Even as I write I can barely fathom the depth of his love and compassion for the people harming him. It is the best love story ever. Even as a little girl I was enthralled. As an adult I still try to attend Good Friday services when I can. So far the most powerful one I've experienced was in Ann Arbor, Michigan, at the Power Center, a huge auditorium, where the story was enacted with full-size crucifixes. If you haven't ever been to a Good Friday service, you are missing something. I guarantee that whatever your faith or nonfaith, you'll feel the love of Jesus down to your bones.

My crush was responding to criticisms of his interpretation of the story. It was too gory. Too one-sided. Too harsh, too this, too that. As I remember it, the interviewer asked how he would respond to someone criticizing his film.

A pause. "I'd forgive them."

Oh, no. The arrogance in his voice told me he had it wrong. It was that I'm-better-than-you tone that gives me goose bumps because it's the same I'm-better-than-you tone that says, "You don't get God because he's ours." In a flash I felt the arrogance that starts wars and splits families and breaks hearts and destroys countries as powerfully as any natural disaster.

I stood there stunned, thinking I had lost him forever. He has it wrong. He doesn't get to decide who is holy and who isn't, and who has the spiritual answers we all yearn for and who doesn't. Still standing in front of the television long after the interview was over, I thought about how much we compromise our own innate intelligence when we look for black-and-white truths in a world that is really a thousand shades of gray. Is he right or wrong? Is she good or bad?

Here's the truth: we're all holy and we all get God if we want God and we all have the spiritual answers we want locked in our own hearts and how do I know because by the time you are reading this I'll have spent more than eighteen years meditating and studying scriptures and living in spiritual abbeys shoveling the dreck off my own heart to see what's at the bottom.

And here's what's there: Beyond a boundaryless spaciousness that tastes of wisdom and compassion, there is a knowing that every single thing and every single person is holy. To double-check myself, because I can get pretty paranoid after only two Diet Cokes and it's been a three-Diet-Cokes-a-day week, I checked in with spiritual leaders from other traditions. They agreed. The Baal Shem Tov, for example, from the Jewish tradition, saw God in every pebble and blade of grass. Jesus took the time to heal lepers who, by definition, were unclean, which meant in his time that touching them should have made him unclean too.

But it didn't. Because they weren't. Everyone is holy. My crush. Me. You. And this is the knowing that could help us all get back on a world peace and let's-share-our-toys track, not arguments about someone's interpretation of the last hours of the life of Jesus.

My crush is holy. And so, after my initial gasp at his interview, I reconnected with my feelings for him. Those blue eyes are worth fighting for. Plus, if I got uppity with my crush, I was being exactly the kind of person I am terrified of becoming—judgmental.

• • •

Back in 1988, finishing the last week of my very first meditation class, I decided to set the goal of becoming fully enlightened before I died. It made sense at the time. Besides, how hard could it be? All I had to do was stare at walls for hours a day when I could, study scriptures, chant a lot, and be nice. I had been raised to be nice, am a bookworm extraordinaire, and was singing to myself all the time already. By 1995 I had spent three years in the Maitreya Buddhist Seminary in Ann Arbor and Toronto, an around-the-clock spiritual boot camp, and had emerged as an ordained Buddhist minister. Calmer, less stressed, no closer to enlightenment. I wrote a book about the seminary, *Stumbling toward Enlightenment,* which my teacher, Venerable Samu Sunim, immediately told me had the wrong title. "Stumbling *into* Enlightenment," he said. That is how this path works. There is no *toward.* We're all already there. We just don't know it. We just have to find a path that will help us fall into enlightenment. His advice was too late. The book was at the printer.

In the ten years since *Stumbling,* I've continued this spiritual work with great fervor. I meditate every day. It isn't anything fancy. I just plunk myself down on a big round cushion, straighten my back, lower my eyes, and breathe in and out, slowly and steadily. On every out-breath I think the question "What is it?"—a question my teacher gave me years ago to focus on. Any number of thoughts could work instead—the word *peace,* for example. Or I could count to ten for ten breaths and then start all over until I'm done meditating.

When I catch myself distracted by thinking, I just go back to the question. After thirty minutes or so I stop, read a scripture, and am ready to stand up and face the day, arms open.

I don't know why I keep sitting, exactly. It just seems to suit me. Plus I've noticed that when I don't take time to sit, a subtle crankiness creeps up my spine, making me less patient with myself and the world at large. It is better to sit for a half hour than to wish crankiness on anyone.

Meanwhile, in a life that is at the same time hilarious and intense, I opened the city of Detroit's first Zen Buddhist Temple in 2000 because it seemed the thing to do. Helped by dozens of people who appeared out of nowhere, Still Point is now a solid and sincere place of refuge for those of us willing to take a good look at how we're living our lives. So we can do better.

After all the years of work, the by-now hundreds of thousands of prostrations, years of meditation, and so much chanting that chants fill my head even in the dentist's chair, where I used to pray for death, I've realized only this: that everything and everyone is precious beyond words. Everything and everyone is holy. And the point of our being on this sweet planet is to be of service to all of it. And when we understand this truth in our bones, joy fills our hearts. I swear it.

This message is a hard sell. We keep looking for labels, you and I. Signs of success. Badges. On some days people want to know only if I'm "enlightened." Given the muddy nature of the word, I always cringe at the question. The last exchange happened as I was preparing to leave Still Point after five years for the life of adventure, one without the protection of abbey walls. On a quiet Tuesday I found myself sitting at the kitchen table staring at my cell phone. It was the third urgent phone call in a week. Each one wore me out because I never knew what the urgency would be when I returned the initial "Please call: urgent" messages that popped up on the phone, mostly in the middle of the night. Sometimes it was a death. Sometimes a lover had just smashed her partner into a wall. When the callers were young, under thirty years old, say, the urgency was often a depression they couldn't shake, nor did they have money for medication, let alone a doctor's visit. "Would meditation help me?" they would ask. "Yes," I'd say, "but I don't know how quickly. Go see a doctor. Do what you have to do to pay for an appointment." In Detroit this can mean selling plasma, prescription drugs, books, CDs.

That week, a so-called vacation week, the phone rang and I couldn't decide whether or not to answer it. The sugar-free, chocolate-covered toffee bar in my mouth was so sticky that most of the teeth on the right side of my mouth were glued together. A good excuse not to answer. Saliva was everywhere. If it had been a video phone the caller would have seen: bare feet with dirt stains on the bottom from being shoeless all the time; old black yoga pants from Bikram days, topped by a hand-me-down T-shirt from my daughter's collection. That day's choice was an old Abercrombie tee with a surfer theme and tan edging at the collar. The clothing was topped by a pleasant female face with intense brown-red eyes and, according to my friend Terry, goofy, sexy curly hair. (He is correct about the goofy part. The sexy part is because he is my friend.)

I picked up the phone and pushed the receiver button. It's a habit I can't break. If I'm in the building I answer every call.

"I'm just wondering. I've heard about you. And I'm just wondering ... are you enlightened?"

Silence. The toffee was hardening in my mouth.

Finally, a garbled response. "Look, I'm just a dharma teacher. Every day I make a vow to be compassionate and wise. Sometimes it works."

Silence again.

By now the toffee was locking onto a temporary crown. My mind was already in a panic, contemplating walking into the dentist's office with a crown in my hand. So much for mindfulness, let alone enlightenment. Beyond the tooth, simply trying to live each minute of this wildly entertaining journey takes up all the gray matter in my head.

Experience has taught me that *enlightenment* has become an empty word. It means whatever the caller or e-mailer or person at the door wants it to mean. To even engage in the conversation about it is harmful to both of us. Every week it seems that someone is e-mailing me with this question. I'm always surprised that they don't ask me about my training instead or how long I've been at this. One time there was an e-mail that came in at 4:40 a.m. The writer had been reading about Buddhism for a couple of years and wanted to start practicing. He was looking for a sangha, a community where he could feel at home. First, though a question: "How many people at Still Point are enlightened?"

I responded, "Well, there's Neptune, the abbey cat...."

He didn't write back. I hadn't given him the head count he wanted. If I'd told him that everyone at Still Point is enlightened, he'd never have believed me. But they are. Some people just don't know it and are stumbling the way I did, the way I do. Some have a sense of awakeness but still don't trust it. Some just plain glow in the dark. Their spiritual energy is palpable. I didn't say any of this in the e-mail. He was asking the wrong question. If he asked me how we all live with the dreck that comes at us every day, then we could talk.

In the stuck-teeth phone call, I experience the same misplaced concern. I can tell my unresponsiveness is making her uncomfortable. "Look," I finally say, as my teeth at last unglue themselves from each other, crown intact. "How do you see the world?"

The woman tells me how overwhelmed she is with Iraq, U.S. politics, school, her husband, her job, traffic. I'm guessing that she is around twenty-five. An East Coaster. Maybe from Boston. I know she is sincere because it isn't easy to track me down and she managed to find my cell phone number.

"Break it down," I tell her. "How do you see your husband?"

Her answer is long. She doesn't much like him. I wonder why they are married.

"He's holy," I say.

She says nothing.

"How about your boss?"

Another long answer. Her concerns sound legitimate. The woman she is describing may be the most unskilled boss on the face of the planet.

"Well ... she's holy too."

The caller doesn't like this answer either. There is silence. This time it is at her end of the line. It feels long. Finally, "Is everyone holy?"

"Yup. This includes your pets, your yard, your car if you have one."

The phone goes dead.

It would have been so much easier for both of us if I'd said I was enlightened, given her the answer she wanted to hear. But I would have been lying. The word is too far away from how I live my life. I don't even know how to think about it anymore. Instead, I've learned the hard way that for those of us determined to measure our progress on the spiritual path, a more helpful test is to ask ourselves a simple question: "Is everything and everyone precious?" Then, if we must have extra points, à la high school, we can ask ourselves, "Is everyone and everything holy?" If the answer is anything but "Of course," we have work to do.

• • •

The question that caught me, thinking about holiness, was this: Given that most of us can't dedicate years of our lives to living in abbeys, is there an obvious way to become so fully present in our lives

that we truly experience the world and everything in it as holy? How
can we get to the place where our lives have the sweetness that this
understanding brings? What would be the factors, the ingredients, if
you will? For the last two years I've thought about this pretty constantly. It's not like people don't pray. Everyone I know prays in some
form. Maybe the form is meditation. Or the Lord's Prayer. Maybe
it takes the form of prostrations toward Mecca or saying rosaries
every day. Fly fishing. My friend Jill prays when she spends full days
transforming people's yards into gardens that could give Monet a run
for his money.

But. Not everyone who prays, whatever the form, experiences the world as holy. If they did, my guess is we'd see the end
of hunger and poverty and racism pretty quickly. Wars would
be only cyberspace games. But most of us, even good people,
don't experience the world in this way. So what is the difference
between those who experience every little thing as precious and
everyone else?

It took hard thinking and a whole lot of meditation before the
answer surfaced, but when it did I knew, *I knew,* the difference was
in our behaviors. I already had a strong sense that this might be true.
And I was fearless about going over old sutras, spiritual teachings, for
clues. The mother lode was the Flower Ornament Sutra, an ancient
collection of teachings related to spiritual growth. I realized that I
was testing out the teachings because I'm ornery enough to want to
experience for myself how things work. I saw that people who actually experience the world as holy (as opposed to talking ourselves into

believing this) behave in specific ways, and these behaviors not only feed each other, they create a deep happiness that can't be bought, not even if your name is Bill Gates.

And here's the best part. You don't need to believe a word of what I'm saying because you can test this teaching out through your own experience. In fact, the Buddha insisted on this. Twenty-five hundred years ago, in the Kalama Sutta, he taught:

1. Do not believe in anything on mere hearsay.

2. Do not believe in traditions merely because they are old and have been handed down for many generations and in many places.

3. Do not believe anything on account of rumors or because people talk a great deal about it.

4. Do not believe because the written testimony of some ancient sage is shown to you.

5. Do not believe in what you have fancied, thinking that because it is extraordinary it must have been inspired by a god or other wonderful being.

6. Do not believe anything merely because presumption is in its favor or because the custom of many years inclines you to take it as true.

7. Do not believe anything merely on the authority of your teachers and priests.

The Chocolate Cake Sutra offers up specific behaviors as a recipe for stumbling into this land of pure sweetness where everything and everyone is precious beyond measure. Chocolate cake is my favorite food in the whole world. It is the reason why I am just about the only person I know who did not go on the South Beach Diet or Atkins. Both are impossibilities given my penchant for starting days with cake no matter the season. Chocolate cake is my high-tea companion, muse, and proof of the possibility of unerring perfection in the world. Chocolate cake is holy.

A melt-in-your-mouth chocolate cake is the perfect metaphor for where we can land if we introduce the correct ingredients into our lives. When the ingredients merge and melt together, we become spiritual warriors, able to take the slings and arrows of planet life in stride, with grace and a grin. The ingredients? Genuine generosity; ethical conduct mixing in whistle-blowing as an art form; extreme tolerance; energetic effort; clearheadedness; opening our arms to crazy wisdom; living life as an adventurer; being a true friend; and bringing so much wisdom to our own tables that we might as well change our middle names to Yoda.

Each ingredient matters. It's like that cake. Without some of the ingredients, you might be able to create an okay cake. But if you use all of them, Betty Crocker herself will smile from the heavens. And while prayer may speed up the baking process, the ingredients work for anyone with a sincere heart. In Detroit. In Auckland. In Pondicherry. In Baghdad. In Seattle.

$\mathscr{P}$reheating the $\mathcal{O}$ven

[A]ll the flowers he has made are beautiful: the rose in its glory, the lily in its whiteness, don't rob the tiny violet of its sweet smell, or the daisy of its charming simplicity. I saw that if all these ... blooms wanted to be roses instead, nature would lose the gaiety of her springtide dress ... so it is with the world of souls, which is his garden.... Perfection consists simply in doing his will, and being just what he wants us to be.

—St. Thérèse of Lisieux

$\mathcal{I}$n 1974, to subsidize graduate school costs, I started an in-home day care center for four little girls, ages one to three. They would show up at my little farmhouse in Oregon promptly at 7:00 each morning. We had a great time cleaning, cooking, and watching *Sesame Street* before our first mininap of the day. After our favorite lunch of peanut butter and homemade jam on fresh-baked whole-grain bread, we would take longer naps and then do arts and crafts until parents started showing up, beginning at 4:30.

Because we spent every weekday together, I got to know the kids and their parents really well. And even though I didn't have formal training in child rearing, growing up as the oldest of five children had taught me the value of (a) structured days, (b) loving the kids no matter what, and (c) naps. It didn't take long for the parents to start asking me for child-rearing advice when they found themselves in an untried parenting situation. I was happy to give it.

One conversation I will remember until my last breath was an early evening phone call from one of the mothers. Her voice sounded exhausted. Apparently Jenny had become hysterical on the bus ride home. Her mom had tried everything to settle her down, but she couldn't stop the tears, even with bribes of favorite foods and extra television. I knew her reaction meant that Jenny was really upset.

"Well, why was she crying?" I asked. "Did she tell you?"

"Yes."

"Then why?"

A silence. Then, "Because George Washington is dead."

Okay, I laughed. I didn't mean to. Then I suggested a couple of children's books about death and dying and told her mom I would be happy to read them to Jenny if she tracked them down.

The books helped, although Jenny is probably still a little sad some thirty years later.

The thing is, I know exactly how she felt. I cry every year when we celebrate Martin Luther King Day. Because he's dead.

The Reverend Martin Luther King Jr. is my all-time hero. His photograph, the one where he is staring out of the Birmingham jail cell, is on my altar, just beside Buddha and across from the Hindu saint Ma Meera. Every day I bow to him and thank him for his great wisdom and compassion.

The Reverend King is holy. Not only did he demonstrate unbelievable courage in the face of constant threats of assassination, he simply refused to fight violence with violence. And he refused to step away from doing what is right, even in the face of rejection by his peers. Perhaps this is demonstrated best in his letter from Birmingham jail. It was written when he was thirty-four years old, and reading it every year on his birthday gives me the courage to keep trucking down this spiritual path. It reminds me of the importance of standing for justice. For speaking our hearts. Here is a small taste:

April 16, 1963

My dear fellow clergymen:

While confined here in the Birmingham city jail, I came across your recent statement calling my present activities "unwise and untimely." Seldom do I pause to answer criticism of my work and ideas. If I sought to answer all the criticisms that cross my desk, my secretaries would have little time for anything other than such correspondence in the course of the day, and I would have no time for constructive work. But since I feel that you are men of genuine good will and that your criticisms are sincerely set forth, I want to answer your statements....

*I am in Birmingham because injustice is here. Just as the
prophets of the eighth century B.C. left their villages and
carried their "thus saith the Lord" far beyond the boundar-
ies of their home towns, and just as the Apostle Paul left his
village of Tarsus and carried the gospel of Jesus Christ to the
far corners of the Greco-Roman world, so am I compelled to
carry the gospel of freedom beyond my home town. Like Paul,
I must constantly respond to the Macedonian call for aid....*

One man. History changed forever. One of the most interesting
things about his life is that much prework went into his maturing
into a holy man. We forget about this sometimes. Born in Atlanta,
Georgia, in 1929, he was the son of a beloved minister, the Reverend
Martin Luther King Sr. He grew up with the gospels of Jesus Christ.
He was admitted to Morehouse College at the age of fifteen, gradu-
ating several years later only to enter Crozier Theological Seminary,
where he was ordained as a Baptist minister at nineteen. His educa-
tion didn't stop there. Dr. King earned his doctorate of philosophy
in systematic theology from Boston University in 1955. So when
Rosa Parks said enough is enough in December of that year, the
Reverend King was primed to step into a leadership role in the civil
rights movement. He had studied theology for years, had thought
about honor and justice for a long time.

He had written about civil rights in *Strive Toward Freedom*
and visited India to study Gandhi's philosophy of nonviolence.
Politically astute, he had made the effort to meet political leaders
and even the president of the United States. The Reverend King was

ready for his role as a warrior for justice, even in the face of stab-
bings and assaults. When he was shot on April 4, 1968, the world
wept. Some of us still do.

• • •

Prework gives us the grounding we need to step into the
experience of daily holiness. In a way it warms our systems up,
creating space for new experiences and helping us to let go of the
things we need to let go of, like resenting our first girlfriend or
boyfriend even though we haven't seen that person for the last, say,
fifteen years. This prework comes in two forms: trusting ourselves,
which includes believing that inside of us is a good person capable
of living a life that is holy, and the practice of gratitude no matter
what life brings.

When I was in the first through fifth grades, my family went
through a hard-core religious phase. We went to church every
Sunday. My sisters and I were sent to a Catholic school. We took
catechism lessons. I loved all of it, mostly because I won the Friday
afternoon spelling bees, which kept me in rosaries until my forties.
And I couldn't believe our luck when we found out that we could
dress up in child-sized wedding dresses, complete with a veil and
patent leather shoes, not once but twice—for First Communion and
Holy Confirmation. And it only got better. I got to choose a saint's
name to stick in between my middle and last names.

The choice was a no-brainer. St. Thérèse of Lisieux was my
woman. St. Thérèse is much beloved. This could be because she
is the patron saint of an enormous variety of people and places.

Here is a partial listing: African missions; AIDS sufferers; aircraft pilots; aviators; bodily ills; the diocese of Fairbanks, Alaska; florists; flower growers; France; illness; orphans; missionaries; religious freedom in Russia; Russia itself; Spanish air crews; and tuberculosis.

I liked her because she was a scrawny little brat, in her own words, "a little imp at four years old" who had the determination of a five-star general. She decided that she wanted to be a nun before she even hit grade school. When she was fifteen and the local priest told her she was still too young, she took her case to the local bishop. When he said no, she convinced her father to take her to Rome to see Pope Leo XIII so she could make her case face-to-face. As soon as she knelt in front of the pope, Thérèse made an eloquent plea for permission to become a nun. When the pope also said no, she wouldn't stop arguing with him, even as his staff literally picked her up off the ground to carry her out of the room.

I loved Thérèse because she trusted herself completely. And she knew in her heart how important behavior can be. In fact, all of her spiritual work centered around simple acts of kindness: she always ate everything she was served without complaint, even though she was often given rotten food once the nuns saw her behavior—just to make sure she was sincere. Once when she was accused of breaking a vase she sank to her knees asking for forgiveness even though someone else had broken it.

In another situation she had to pray every evening in a pew right in front of a nun who made "a strange little noise which resembled the noise one would make when rubbing two shells, one against another." It drove Thérèse nuts, partly because her hearing was so sensitive, partly because the other nun didn't even know she was doing it, and partly because it happened regularly.

Sometimes the sound would bother the young nun so much that she would break out into a sweat trying to ignore it. Finally she just leaned into the sound, grateful for the opportunity to watch her own reaction, "and my prayer was spent in offering this concert to Jesus."

I wonder, How many of us could pull that off? Maybe on a good day, like a day after a retreat I might. But over and over, every day? Not likely.

Even Thérèse had prework. It didn't hurt that her mother wanted to be a saint and her father a monk. Rumor has it that early in their marriage they vowed to be celibate, until a local priest told them that is not how God wanted marriage to work. The couple ended up having nine children. Five lived, all girls. Thérèse was born in Alençon, France, on January 2, 1873. Partly because of her parents' religious habits, by the time she was two she decided that she loved the Catholic Church and wanted to be a part of it. Her parents took her to church regularly, and after her mother died when she was four years old, she was raised by older sisters who were all headed for nunneries. Thérèse was immersed in and com-forted by the Catholic Church. On her daily walks with her father they visited churches. Often her father would also give her money to give to the poor people they met along the way.

Life wasn't easy for Thérèse. Not only did she lose her
mother when she was small, but she was also abandoned by her
big sisters as they headed off one by one to become Carmelite
nuns. In grade school the young girl almost died from a disease
whose symptoms included constant headaches with constant
shaking and delirium when she wasn't in a comalike state. Convinced she was dying, Thérèse prayed to Mary, the mother of
Jesus, and was healed. As a result of her suffering Thérèse then
knew that life, "when you saw it as it really was, just meant con-
tinual suffering."

As a pint-sized smart aleck with a fast tongue, Thérèse faced
bullies in and out of school. No matter, she took the hits and kept
going, at one point wearing a large crucifix tucked into her belt like
other martyrs.

By the time Thérèse finally made it into a convent setting, she
was primed for sainthood. In her writings you can feel her radiance, her deep compassion, and her determination to be of help to
the world. For Thérèse, everything and everyone was holy. Period.
Even though she died from tuberculosis at the age of twenty-four,
the young woman had such an impact on those who knew her that
there was an immediate call for canonization. Reflections growing
out of her spirited radiance are used for guidance and comfort to
this day. Plus, I'll bet that there are a million of us by now who have
taken her name to remind ourselves that her experience can be our
experience. Perfect flowers all.

. . .

If renowned spiritual teachers made good use of prework, so can we. Every five years or so my clothes get tight. This includes the baggy black jeans I bought in Paris in 1988. When I look down at my body to see why, there are always (sigh) about fifteen pounds that weren't there before my clothes felt tight. The first few times it happened I pretty much convinced myself that evil gnomes had snuck into my bedroom at night and shoved globules of fat into my thighs, belly, butt, and upper arms.

While the fat itself never struck me as particularly ugly, I'm too cheap to buy new clothes just because the old ones don't fit. Also, by the time I reached the ripe old age of forty I knew from experience that I didn't have the staying power to lose the weight on my own. It was just too hard. So I signed up with Weight Watchers. And loved it.

Keeping lists of what I ate each day reminded me of grade school. Tangible evidence of effort. I even went out and bought gold stars to put under the dates of days when I stayed the Weight Watcher course. Mostly these were days when I managed to drink the full-sized fish aquarium's worth of water that seemed to be critical to the weight-loss regime. Since I hate drinking water, it was certainly the toughest part for me.

Invariably, after about three months, or less than that if I was headed for a vacation somewhere near big water or to a friend's second wedding, the fifteen pounds would go away. The baggy jeans would be baggy again. I'd stop paying attention to what I was eating and go back to a glass or two of water a day.

The weight would come back. So I'd head for Weight Watchers, lose the pounds. Leave my bedroom light on to catch those bastard gnomes. And the cycle would kick in again.

After the third round of this dance I finally stayed after one of our weekly cheerleader-led meetings to ask that evening's cheerleader what I was doing wrong. She assured me that the answer was nothing. (Oh, how I love those Weight Watcher women!) Then she suggested that we do a quick review of my behavior patterns, starting with the prework I did before I signed up each time.

"Prework?"

"Yeah, like cleaning out your cupboards and refrigerator of the foods that aren't good for you."

She pulled out a sheet of paper and started scribbling things down. Here are the ones I remember: Putting lots of bottles of water on the top shelf of the refrigerator so I could just grab "a cold one" whenever I felt like it. Cutting up vegetables and putting them in see-through containers so I'd grab them as well. Throwing out my secret stashes of Godiva chocolate—the boxes I hide in the lettuce drawer of the refrigerator since I never buy lettuce. (It only rots and then goes to compost.) The Ben & Jerry's behind the frozen broccoli in the freezer. Even the trail mix had to go unless I was willing to pull the M&Ms out and give them away.

She wasn't done. I needed to buy a new pair of running shoes and set them by the door next to a sweatshirt and umbrella so it would be easy for me to head outside for a spontaneous walk at any time.

She told me that people didn't realize how much success in keeping weight off depended on the prework—having good-for-you foods easily available, the right gear for going outside to exercise, rain or shine. Belief in yourself. Especially that.

"You can do this," she said. "You already have a couple of times. Let's see what the prework does."

It kept the weight off. That's what it did. I kid you not. It was the only thing I changed in my most recent three-month weight-loss effort. That was a while back, and those baggy jeans are still baggy.

Faith in Ourselves . . . and in Each Other

Prework starts with faith. Faith in ourselves matters. Some of us have to learn the hard way that in the end the only person whose opinion matters is our own. Everyone else is responding to us through their own karmic screens. I learned this the hard way when I gave a speech for Michigan's governor. I worked for Jim Blanchard when I was in my early thirties. Although I started out in his Cabinet Council, I ended up working for the Department of Commerce. It was a job I loved—mostly working with entrepreneurs. I also started speaking in front of community and business groups. One night I was asked to take the governor's place before an auditorium full of businessmen furious with his policies. When I appeared in his stead, they were fit to be tied. They wanted to hear from the governor, not an underling. I did my best, deciding, even as I stood at the podium, that they hated me.

At the end of the speech I barely managed to make it to the back of the room without crying. There was a public phone just outside the door. I picked it up to call in my resignation. Happily, the governor's chief of staff was still at the office. When he finally understood what I was trying to tell him through tears that would no longer wait, he just laughed. This was not quite the reaction I expected. Then he said, "Forget it. We won't accept your resignation. And you aren't fired. Don't you know that no matter what you do, half the world will think you're an asshole?"

As soon as he said it I knew he was right. And started paying better attention to my own gut reactions to people, places, and things.

Faith in ourselves matters. The Buddha was forever teaching this. So have all the legitimate teachers who followed in his footsteps. Even as an old man, when he was dying a painful death and his monks kept pestering him to name a successor, he flat-out refused. "You be your own lamps," he said. And that was that.

I honestly believe that if I asked just about anyone who has shown up to meditate with me if they have faith in themselves they would say yes. But we don't. We lock on to leaders and trust their words even as their behavior heads in a different direction.

Here is just one story to demonstrate. A great master spent years training several hundred disciples. One day he called them into the great hall. After reviewing the spiritual traditions of wisdom and compassion, he announced that it was now time for his followers to demonstrate their loyalty to him. Each was to go out of the temple and kill one thing—a plant, an animal, or a person—and bring it back to him.

All of the disciples rushed from the room to do his bidding. All except one.

He was a quiet young man who had always done as instructed. In fact, he had studied with the great master from the time he was five years old. As soon as the room emptied he walked up to the old monk.

"I quit!" he shouted. "How can you preach loving-kindness and that everything is sacred and then turn right around and instruct people to harm? You are a fraud!"

The old man stared at him. Then he smiled. "Finally, I've found my successor."

Fortunately, the rest of the disciples were called back before any damage was done.

It sounds so easy, this faith in ourselves. I've always been a smart mouth. Talked back to my teacher in the seminary when I disagreed with him. Once or twice I even yelled back. It never occurred to me that I didn't have complete faith in myself.

But then I discovered koans, those seemingly meaningless questions that many of us Buddhist types are drawn to. "What is Buddha's original face?" is one. "Does a dog have Buddha nature?" is another. I also discovered Barbara Rhodes, Zen master Soeng Hyang, in the Kwan Um School of Zen Buddhism. A spunky, small woman, she is a warrior's warrior. Fearlessly honest. A hospice

nurse who lights up a room with her grin, she is no-nonsense, this
Zen master. In 2001 I asked for permission to attend my first long
retreat with her so I could practice koans. In my earlier training
with Venerable Samu Sunim, a Korean Zen master, he had always
told me that once I understood the response to the question "What
is it?" all koans could be answered. Although I was pretty sure I
believed him, I still wanted to see for myself if it was true.

In the first retreat with Soeng Hyang, we flew through a half
dozen koans. "All Dharmas return to one. Where does one return?" A
watch was plunked down between us in the interview room. "Please
respond. If you say it is a watch, wrong. If you say it is not a watch,
wrong." I loved it. I loved it because she was forcing spontaneous
responses. Without time to think, I could see what the real me was
like. I could see if I simply responded or tried to second-guess myself.
I could see if I was willing to let my own response surface or try to
give her what I thought she wanted.

The second retreat, a year later, was much harder. I had spent
a year koan-question-free. It took a couple of days to settle down to
where I was fully present for the questions. One that caught me was,
"How do you greet a master in the road without words or silence?"
I responded. Soeng Hyang told me I was wrong. I tried something
else. She rang me out of the room.

The next day we tried it again. I responded. She said wrong.
Then she really yelled at me. "How can you be a guiding teacher
for a Zen Buddhist temple and not trust yourself?" She sounded

really angry. In that instant I could see where I still didn't fully trust myself, and I vowed not to make that mistake again. I remembered how critical it is to trust our reactions to situations, people, and animals. She asked again. How would I greet a master in the road? I spontaneously responded. She said I was wrong and asked me again. I simply repeated my response, knowing that was exactly how I would greet anyone, including a Zen master. Without a reaction, she moved on to the next question. Since then, every time I catch myself beginning to second-guess a decision I've made, I think of Soeng Hyang and do a little bow of gratitude for the time she shared with me.

This faith in myself made it possible to be forthright with a man I dated last fall. In my gut, I knew we were a match on many levels—a PhD monk who used to do modern dance with a PhD scientist who does improv. Tell me it isn't a match. Also he is very good-looking, which totally appealed to my superficial self. But I just wasn't ready to date. So I stopped. Maybe we'll be friends by the time you read this book.

There is so much to learn about having faith in ourselves. Even with all the mistakes we make, people are good. This includes you and me. I see it all the time.

I remember driving the fifty or so miles from Ann Arbor to Detroit in one of those winter storms that makes us all stop what we're doing to pray for sun. Half snow, half freezing rain, the conditions were pretty close to a complete white-out. The roads were such a mess that every highway between Ann Arbor and Detroit had a major accident blocking traffic.

I decided to take a local road east, Michigan Avenue, figuring that even if it took me two and a half hours to get to Detroit (which it did), at least I'd always be moving. About an hour into the drive I stopped at a red light where Michigan Avenue crosses Interstate 275. Standing at the light with his back to me was a man in overalls and a knit cap holding up a sign I couldn't read. I watched as the young woman in the first car in line beeped him over and handed him her sack lunch. When he ran back across the traffic, the next car in line beeped him over. A man's hand stretched out the side window. This time it was money.

As I waited, *every single car* in that line gave him something. Food. Money. What looked like a bottle of Tide. Complete strangers. Men and women. Black and white. All ages. That goodness is there. We just need to trust it.

Gratitude

And then there is gratitude. That gratitude helps to kickbox our spiritual selves into gear comes as a surprise to a lot of people. It helps more than we know, sort of like oil spilled on a fire.

Every once in a while my Explorer Scout gene gets the better of me. Sometimes it gets me into trouble. When I was sixteen I decided that I needed to know what it felt like to jump off a not-too-high bridge into a river. There happened to be a not-too-high bridge on Cape Cod where I was nannying three little boys. Even better, a boy

I met on the beach agreed to drive a hearse filled with friends to the bridge in the middle of traffic so we could leap into the river.

It never occurred to us that there might be boats under the bridge. There were. I barely missed a huge sailboat. Hitting the water, I could have touched the boat with my left hand. As soon as we surfaced and counted heads to make sure we had all survived our great leap of pure stupidity, we knew we were in trouble. I could hear the sirens even as I swam across the river. I'm sure the only reason we weren't arrested, given the monumental traffic jam we created, was that none of us, hearse included, crossed that bridge again for the entire summer.

That experience, exhilarating and terrifying in the same breath, began a behavior pattern of pushes to the edge of experience—just to see what it would be like—that has never stopped, although happily there is more and more time between the I-wonder-what-it-would-feel-like and the actual trying-out. Luckily, I never took to alcohol or drugs or I'd be dead by now.

Every once in a while that same hunger drives me to do a killer meditation retreat simply to see where it will lead. One January I decided to do a solo seven-day retreat. This was the structure of the days:

4:00 a.m.	Wake up
4:30 a.m.	250 prostrations to the ground
	Chanting
	Meditation for 30 minutes followed by a 10-minute break

Repeat the prostrations through the day until 1000 are completed.
Surround them with sitting meditation, some study, walking, juice,
and soup.

10:00 p.m.   Lights out

4:00 a.m.   Repeat above pattern

In addition to the structure, I decided to do a juice fast for
the first three days to kick into meditation mode faster.

For the first twenty-four hours it was heaven. Sittings were
strong, and I was delighted to be away from the Internet and
constant phone calls. Fruit juice has always fallen just behind
dark chocolate as a food group I could live on forever and ever. By
the second day, however, things started going downhill. First off,
the combination of juicing and prostrations made me so giddy I
became a one-woman Teletubbie. My brain kept wanting to sing,
"Joy to the World." Everything I saw was either desperately beautiful or breathtakingly funny. None of this was helping my concentration. Second, the combination of juice and prostrations meant
that I fell asleep in full sitting position at about 8:00 p.m. Not wob-
bly almost-asleep. Snoring, dream-filled sleep. The kind that takes
you into and through the night.

So I gave up on the juice and introduced protein into meals
in the form of peanut butter, cheese, and eggs ... and added homemade french fries for grounding.

Heading into day three, the whining started. "This is stupid."
"No, this is stupid and too hard." "This is stupid, too hard, and

wrecking my legs." On and on through the first sitting until for some reason that I will never understand, this thought surfaced: "I am so grateful for the refrigerator."

Following a flash of, "Oh, now I'm completely nuts. It has finally happened," was a rush of, "The weather is perfect. Cold and clear." (It was seven degrees below zero.) By the time I caught the thoughts and went back to my meditation practice, I felt rested, balanced, and quiet.

Two hours later, more resistance. I needed to check my e-mail, to call the hospice to see how Mary was doing, to get some soup out of the freezer. As waves of thinking started building momentum, a pause. Then gratitude again. "I'm so lucky to be able to do this, to have limbs that work, a roof over my head." From that moment on, every time whining or worrying started to surface, I picked something random to be grateful for. In the process I suddenly realized how powerful simple gratitude is. It can slice though all sorts of egomania, and it slices quickly. Irritation. Worry. Fear. Depression. You name it. Gratitude is a frigging sword.

Finishing the retreat I wrote a list of everything in my life I'm grateful for. At the end of five single-spaced pages, I realized that I had no excuse to whine about anything—including death—because this life has given me, has given us, a huge opportunity to grow spiritually in all sorts of unimaginable ways. I was even grateful for the leg cramps and that mostly I don't get them. For the first time in my life I understood why a few people I have known who faced unbearable diseases—leukemia, brain tumors, ALS—told me that they were grateful for the diseases because their situations forced them into living their lives honestly, to shed the stuff that just didn't matter (pretty much everything outside of their relationships with other people), and to appreciate everything from a flower in a vase to a simple hug.

Even with societal sanctions to be bitter, depressed, despondent, or just plain mean, these were people who glowed. Looking back, I see that gratitude was their secret ingredient—way more powerful than acceptance.

• • •

Gratitude means giving up whining. We whine so much. I wonder how long this has been true. So what if life is hard? It is also glorious, educational, and hilarious. We get a chance to work off negative karma. Yet more and more I hear us focusing on the hard parts. Maybe it is my penchant for listening to people on their cell phones. The way I see it, if you are on your cell phone having a conversation I can hear, I get to listen. Last week I tallied the conversations, and here is the breakdown from twenty overheard calls:

Whining	76%
Planning/reminding	7%
Mushy, I-love-you stuff	10%
I couldn't quite hear	1%
Checking in on a child, partner, pet	6%

Whining won, hands down.

I myself love whining. It's just that I've learned, as an Eagle Scout watching the workings of my own brain, that it never helps anything. Not only does it not improve a situation, it just makes me crankier and tires the person I am whining at. That person already has enough on his or her plate just by being alive.

Maybe a dozen years ago I explored the coast of China with a friend. We spent much of the time between cities sailing on a fancy cruise ship. Because she was a pale beauty and I knew something about China, we were invariably invited to join the "in crowd" tables at dinner. These were tables of multimillionaires and famous people and intellectuals who were friends to both groups. While I can remember only one conversation—a Florida-based entrepreneur asked my friend if her pubic hairs were also blond (a quick indicator of how much alcohol was consumed each night)—I do remember the tenor of each night. It was whining. There was too much food or the wrong kind of food. Too much noise outside the cabins. The wrong entertainment. Too many stops on the coast or not enough stops or the wrong stops. All of us were whining—while we were being treated like gods. At the time I was so embarrassed by all of us that I vowed to stop whining forever.

Returning to Ann Arbor, I announced to my unsuspecting preteen daughter that our whining days were done. She looked me over and ignored me, knowing that I often forget such noble intentions following a couple of good nights' sleep. Sure enough, within the week we were both whining to beat the band. I tried everything I could to get us to stop—a point system, small tangible rewards for measurable periods free from whining (Barbie clothes mostly)—but nothing worked.

Finally a homoeopathic solution surfaced. We would cure
whining with whining! A whining hour was instituted. Every
evening from five to six we could only whine. If the phone rang or
a friend showed up, they were instantly introduced to the remedy.
Within three weeks it was over. We had stopped. Where there used
to be whining, there was now either quiet or a thank-you for something. While we both fall back into whining occasionally, given the
deep roots of habit, mostly we don't. And mostly we're grateful for
our lives and all their wild and wonderful components. Life became
measurably easier, calmer, and more sane from this single shift.

Prework. Faith in ourselves. Gratitude. Faith allows us to
stay open to all of the experiences that show up on our doorstep
because we know we'll do our best, no matter what, and we know
that our best is pretty capable. Gratitude keeps us focused on the
world outside of ourselves. We start to see and then to feel all of the
gifts coming our way every minute. Sunshine. Beautiful clouds.
Birds. The mailman. An e-mail from a friend. A cup of tea. We are
laying the groundwork for a sweet, sweet life, from our breath to
our thoughts, a life in which Mel fits, and our best friend fits, and
our former best friend fits, and so does everyone and everything
in between. This simple acceptance, all by itself, makes us ready to
start mixing the rest of the ingredients into a life that rocks, plain
and simple. From a spiritual maturity perspective, faith and gratitude create fertile soil for the specific behaviors that can transform
our experience of every day to one of deep happiness, laced with
energy ... without a Red Bull.

THE FIRST INGREDIENT:
Joy

Those who perform good deeds
do not experience remorse and woe.
Instead
they are happy now
and they are happy later—
in this world
and the next
they know bliss.

—The Buddha

’m in Seattle for two weeks looking for a place to live. Suddenly fried clam necks are in all my dreams. Therapist friends would have a field day with this. I’ve had fried clam strips at least five times since I’ve been here, a personal record. It has been a long time since I’ve had access to so much hot, greasy, salty nuttiness in one bite. Better than toffee, closing in on chocolate cake.

Right now I'm sitting at a tiny corner table in a family-owned café close to the locks—they sell only fried fish, chicken, chips, and drinks. A gallon-sized tip jar on the counter has a sign, Karma Jar, on it. The jar is almost full, so their karma must be pretty good.

Halfway through more fried clams than I've ever eaten in one sitting a family comes in—mom, dad, two little girls. They order lunch then pull out a VISA to pay for it. The café doesn't take VISA. They also won't take a traveler's check. "Too many fakes." Between the two of them, the dad and mom don't have enough cash to pay for the meal.

Within minutes everyone in the café is watching to see what the owners will do. The mom, visibly embarrassed, asks if they will take a personal check; she has plenty of identification. "No checks."

The dad heads off to find an ATM machine, only to come back empty-handed. The money they had transferred into their account hasn't surfaced yet. We all hear the parents talking, voices raised.

They're screwed.

By now there are sixteen of us watching. The girls see their chicken and fries on the counter, ready to eat. The family behind the counter looks down.

I hesitate for a minute. I don't have a job or even a home, for that matter. But how much can a lunch here cost? Walking up to the mother, I tell her, "I have some cash." I'm afraid she will start crying, she looks so relieved. They only need seventeen dollars. She insists on writing me a check for the money. It says twenty dollars.

They get their food and sit down next to me. The mom introduces herself and asks if I've ever been to their town.

"No."

After some quiet she looks at me again. "People are good."

I agree and realize that I'm happier than she is about the whole incident. Why does it feel so good to be generous? Those Karma Jar folks missed a real opportunity to feel what I walked out feeling. Lucky, lucky me.

• • •

Four months earlier I knew that my last day at Still Point Zen Buddhist Temple would be July 31, 2005. It mattered to me that people coming to the temple identify with the teachings and not with a specific teacher. Plus, Koho Vince Anila, my longtime friend and dharma brother, was ready for me to step aside so he could take over. Moving into his thirties, he has the youth, smarts, courage, and spiritual energy that Detroit needs.

Throughout my tenure I expected to move back to Ann Arbor from Detroit. That way I would still be within driving distance of Still Point if they needed me or I needed them. I even had two new jobs in the works, one as a gardening assistant to a brilliant intuitive gardener from England, and the other as a possible sales-clerk in a wonderful downtown garden shop. What I never expected to do was move across the country.

Yet three mornings following the end of our last five-day summer retreat together I woke up with one thought: "Move to Seattle." It's not that I don't love Seattle, it's that I just never again expected to give away everything but my books and paintings so I could put down roots in a new place.

As I sat with the thought of moving I realized that by the time the thought had surfaced fully formed, it was a done deal. So I packed up and started driving. By the end of day one I was tired of CDs and even Harry Potter. Missing Detroit already, I asked myself what the city had taught me. The answer was a surprise. Not that people are good; I knew that. Not that life sucks a lot of the time; I knew that too. Detroit had taught me the behaviors that lead to this life in which I get to see the divine—or God or whatever label you need to use—in the eyes of everyone, infusing everything. It had taught me joy.

In Buddhism we accept that there are ten thousand sorrows in every life. At the same time there are ten thousand joys. In the Dhammapada, a much-beloved sutra, the teaching is clear: "Live in joy." For the more than forty years that he taught, the Buddha focused on behaviors that would pull us toward joy if we acted on the teachings. Generosity is the behavior that starts the joy parade. Generosity is the practice of giving joy.

Maybe I would have figured out the behaviors without Detroit. I doubt it, given my inherent laziness. It took the rawness and intensity of the Midwest to push me past meditation in all its forms. It took the city to clarify the specific behaviors that feed transformation. Starting out on day one of the drive from Detroit to Seattle, I had a sense of this. And 2,342.39 miles later, I'd stake all the rest of my lives on it. We can nurture our own spiritual maturity through specific behaviors.

Generosity

The first one is generosity. Every major spiritual tradition is filled with stories of generosity. Muhammad's caring acts toward the people of his time. Sufi love poems. The Good Samaritan. In Buddhism, the Jataka tales are a collection of stories about the lives Buddha lived before he showed up on the planet as Shakyamuni Buddha. As the story goes, about halfway through the night that Buddha fell into complete enlightenment, he saw all of his past lives. Over the next forty years he occasionally told these stories to clarify particular teachings. Many of them had to do with generosity. His tales were popular enough to show up both on the Indian continent (in Sanskrit) and in Tibet thousands of years after he was physically gone. Their lessons are clear enough for children to understand and moving enough for adults to remember.

One of the most powerful stories of generosity is about a Brahman teenager. In one of his lifetimes Buddha was born into a family of Brahmans who were known as a kind and spiritual clan. His was a good life. He was gorgeous, had money, and was well known and much loved. He was also so wise that people came to him for advice, even when he was young. This included the elder statesmen of the clan.

One day the young Brahman was walking up a mountain trail with his good friend Ajita. They suddenly heard a huge roar coming up from the ravine beside the trail. Looking down, the two saw a young tigress. She was so thin that it was clear she was starving to death. Exhausted and delirious, she was looking strangely at her newborn cubs. In a flash the young men realized that she was going to eat them. The two men watched, fascinated and horrified, as her young cubs moved toward her to suckle.

The tigress was so crazed that she growled at the babies as though she didn't know them. Then she quietly waited as they approached her.

The two men looked at each other. Buddha said to Ajita, "We must quickly find the tigress some food before she kills her babies." He promised to divert the tiger until his friend returned with something to eat. As soon as Ajita sped off, Buddha looked down at the tigress and in one motion threw himself into the ravine. Landing near the tiger, he cut his skin with a stone so she could smell his blood. An instant later she fell on him, eating him instead of her children.

When Ajita returned he saw Buddha being eaten. Although he was overwhelmed and heartbroken, he vowed to be generous for the rest of his life in honor of his friend's selfless act.

As extreme as this story is, I thought about it often during the great drive west, not because I'm planning to throw myself down some ravine but because it gives me a "true north" for generosity. If Buddha can give up his life, the least I can do is share my income, my food, my clothes, my time, my heart.

Word on the street is that Shakyamuni Buddha refused to teach anyone who wasn't genuinely generous first. In one sutra, a king who has given away buildings' worth of food asks him how much merit he has gained. The Buddha's answer? "None." Why? Because the king was only generous in order to look good. It wasn't genuine. What Buddha was after was ego-free generosity. A deeper form of sharing. He wanted people to give away more than they thought they could—time, money, shelter, job leads, and the best Web site for meeting potential mates.

• • •

Almost twenty years ago I placed a little notice on a bulletin board at what was the Chinese Studies Center at the University of Michigan, asking for a tutor in Chinese. Starstruck by my first taste of Buddhism, I wanted to find out if there was an underbelly to the tradition. The teachings seemed too good to be true. I wasn't finding any hints of trouble in English-language books. I figured if I knew Chinese, I could look up the teachings I was reading at the Ann Arbor Zen Buddhist Temple, translate them, discover that Herman Hesse had made up the whole Siddhartha story, and go back to my Unitarian Universalist life in peace.

Mr. Kung responded to my notice in the first week. Within days we were working through a Chinese-language workbook together. Now in his eighties, Mr. Kung is a spry Chinese man whose eyes light up at every little thing. Over the years he has convinced me that the Chinese versions of the teachings match the English versions and that there are no secret scandals, even if I look for anagrams, read the teachings upside down, or rewrite passages backward. Buddha is for real, and the teachings are consistent. More than this, Mr. Kung has taught me about genuine generosity.

I'd show up at his tiny apartment for a lesson, only to be invited to enjoy a three- or four-course meal. He would insist that I take the leftovers—and then refuse to take any payment for the lesson. And that was just the beginning. For the five years I was at Still Point, he gave me at least a box of food each week to take to Detroit from Ann Arbor. One typical week it was two boxes of cornflakes, two loaves of bread, celery, tomatoes, over two dozen tortillas, and a huge bag of clothes for children—mostly hip pants for preteen boys and training bras for preteen girls.

Sometimes the collection of goodies could get pretty funny: cases of milk; a freezer's worth of cheese. All this from a man with no money. When I was ordained as a dharma teacher he gave the temple a beautiful antique jade urn. When I went on a pilgrimage to Korea he gave me one hundred dollars to give to my teacher to help with the trip's expenses. When I needed root canal work and had no insurance, he conjured up one thousand dollars to help pay for it. And while I always got a kick out of seeing what he was offering, his was the greater pleasure. Mr. Kung was always so delighted to be giving me something that he usually ended up laughing out loud. Me too.

· · ·

Generosity feels good even in situations in which we find ourselves giving away something we didn't intend to part with, ever.

During our first three years in Detroit I would walk down its main street, Woodward Avenue, for a dozen blocks to get to our bank. Each time, I passed a homeless man who camped out on one of the adult-sized heating vents on the sidewalk. There was one refrigerator-sized cardboard box for his clothes and one for food and everything else. He kept his bedding, complete with what looked like a brand-new comforter and pillow, on the vent to keep them dry and warm.

I was struck by the sight of him when I first passed by, partly because of the combination of neatness and completeness of his arrangement and partly because he was—okay, I admit it— gorgeous. Think of George Clooney at thirty with very curly hair. That gorgeous.

In Detroit we greet each other on the street. Friends, strangers, everybody. So he and I always said good morning to each other. After a few weeks we began to exchange a few sentences. By the end of the first autumn I was bringing him granola bars each time I saw him. He'd tell me some of the wildest street stories I'd ever heard—drug exchanges; abandoned cars, pets, children. It's amazing what you see when you spend your days camping out on an inner-city sidewalk. I still don't know why he was there, he was so clearheaded. Maybe he was some sort of a psychology-class plant. Wayne State University is right up the street.

One day he was there without the cardboard boxes or the bedding. It was cold—November. In the night someone had taken everything while he was asleep. He figured it was the cops.

I told him I'd go back to the abbey to get him some things.

"Nah. Just give me your sweatshirt."

He was staring at my favorite, faded to just-the-perfect-shade-of-green hooded sweatshirt. I'd had it all my adult life. It had seen me through graduate school, marriage, Europe, Australia, and childbirth. It was my Bunky, my grown-up pacifier, my lucky sweatshirt. I'd even worn it to bed sometimes when I was too tired to change clothes or slightly too cold to get to sleep without an extra layer.

He wanted my favorite green sweatshirt.

I'm quite skilled at giving things away, known for it, even. Every week I give at least a painting or a book to someone. I've given away all of my clothes except for a handful of things (per advice from Oprah) that "give me joy." I don't have any jewelry to speak of.

The man wanted my Bunky.

"Why?"

"Because it smells good."

"You want my favorite sweatshirt in the whole world because it smells good?"

"Yeah. And it's fucking cold out here."

I sighed. Took the sweatshirt off. Handed it to him. Walked away waiting for the tears to come. Instead I felt elated. Thrilled, even. Happy for both of us. That's what generosity does, the real kind. And, okay, I miss it sometimes, but giving it away was the right thing to do.

A few weeks later when I saw him without it he told me someone had stolen it. "My favorite thing in the whole world," he said. We just looked at each other and started laughing.

• • •

Genuine giving feeds joyfulness. The more generosity, the greater joy. And we can be more generous than we ever thought

possible. Polly Miller is my friend and accountant. She takes wonderful care of her clients, friends, and staff. She's a worker's worker,
and I have never seen her away from her office unless we sneak
away for a lunch somewhere after tax season. About five years ago
Polly's husband, Jim, fell off their roof when he was cleaning out
their gutters. He landed on his head. Jim's concussion was so bad
that everyone, including his doctors, thought he would die. Polly
didn't. As soon as she found out what was wrong, she went into
hyperdrive. She demanded extra care for him and got it. She paid
for special therapists and emerging treatments and ignored the rest
of us when we said, "Let him go." I remember sitting in his room at
the hospital, chanting, and then reading to him even though he was
in a coma and wondering if Polly had any idea what she was getting
into. Staying with him at the hospital alone gave her at least one
official sainthood scout badge. What more could she give?

It turns out that she gave him back a life.

When he finally got out of the hospital, Jim could barely
function. Polly had her house reconstructed so he would have room
for all the equipment he needed. She then proceeded to drive him
to specialized rehabilitation programs, not to mention the extra
daily therapy she paid for out of her own pocket. Watching her
determination gave me the energy I needed to keep fighting the
good fight in Detroit on the toughest days. It reminded me, every
time I saw her, that heroes are all around us, that each of us is a
hero if we have the courage to admit it to ourselves. Polly teaches
this to every single person who meets her and hears her story. And

while she looks tired sometimes, Polly is happy with her decision. She has her husband.

· · ·

It is an honor to be surrounded by genuinely generous people. I have no idea how I lucked into it. My friend Ango Neil Heidrich gives things away at every turn. Last Thanksgiving he responded to a woman *who called the wrong number looking for food for her family* by making up a Thanksgiving meal for her and her children. He has been known to drive around Detroit giving people fresh loaves of bakery bread "just because." Two weeks ago he gave our friend Claudia his favorite-in-the-whole-world green couch because she needed one. Every week I used to see Koho Vince Anila giving something away—books, hiking equipment, CDs, clothes. One of these days the man will show up stark naked, I swear. Or there is my friend Mary, who lost almost everything but her breathing thanks to ALS. For one of my birthdays she came up with four (four!) books about wedding protocol for me because she knows that weddings are my favorite thing in the whole world. Now I should be able to crash just about any kind of wedding without getting caught. I have no idea how she pulled it off, but pull it off she did, making me laugh so hard that my stomach was still sore a week later.

One of Still Point's abbey residents, Buddhimant Noel Kulik, bakes cookies every Valentine's Day. We're talking days of baking here, those huge, old-fashioned sugar cookies some of us dream about in our sleep. Not only does she bake them, she also takes the time to frost each one, complete with little heart designs and sprinkles. Think of the fanciest cookies you have ever seen in an expensive bakery. They are like that.

Once the cookies cool down and the frosting hardens, Noel wraps them individually, only to give every single one away to friends, colleagues, and complete strangers.

Then there is MJ. When Mary Jane Hilker lived in the abbey she used to keep us in coffee we could otherwise never afford. And she would bring home chocolate, good chocolate, regularly. It was so hilarious to be living in a tough inner-city neighborhood, trying to make ends meet, and see a fresh box of Godiva chocolates sitting on the kitchen table waiting to be eaten by whoever walked by. On the most miserable, freezing winter night in the winter of 2003–04, when we were up to our eyeballs in crises—deaths, sick preemie babies, a suicide—she packed us all up and took us out for a Korean feast that will forever be one of the best meals of my life. As happy as we were to be eating it, MJ was happier making the meal possible. Her twinkling eyes gave her away.

My mother has always had these tendencies, which is probably why I'm so touched by the wide-openness of this form of generosity. From the time I was a little kid, my mother was available, not only to me but to all my friends. She simply said yes to sharing herself with us. When I came home from school one day—it had to be in second or third grade—and told her about all of the cracks and missing parts on the Mary and Jesus statues around the school, she immediately offered to patch and repaint them. Unfortunately, as a non-Catholic she wasn't fully familiar with the appropriate colors for Catholic statue robes. After their initial shock when the statues were returned, the nuns pretty quickly got over the bright hues of orange and brown.

Later, whenever I was given a detention and she agreed with me that it was unfair, she would show up after school with me. For years she volunteered to teach poetry to women living in public housing. To this day she teaches art to senior citizens and loves it. And they love her.

· · ·

The benefits of genuine generosity are huge. To start with, this kind of giving can provide an immediate escape from the blues. In Detroit the winter of 2004–05 sucked. The downward spin started with the presidential election, for which people turned out in droves—including middle-aged adults voting for the first time—to vote for Kerry, only to watch him lose. As for the city itself, by March 2005 it was facing a $93 million deficit from 2003–04 with a projected $65 million shortfall for 2004–05. Since then the shortfall has grown to some $300 million. Whole neighborhoods didn't even have public lighting. The mayor, Kwame Kilpatrick, was falling fast in popularity: "We have an impoverished core city led by an immature and self-indulgent mayor" (Jack Lessenberry, *Metro Times*, Feb. 23, 2005). Pollution, violence, increases in petty crime throughout the neighborhood, and threats of 160 school closings made us all cranky. And that was just the political environment we were living in. That we had almost constant snow and temperatures in the single digits well into March just added to our collective blues. In my close circle of friends, two "solid" marriages crumbled, a friend's brother committed suicide, and we all got sick. On top of it all my friend Mary, who suffered from Lou Gehrig's disease, was moved an hour's drive away to a hospice center that made me weep whenever I walked through its doors. There is so much sadness there. You walk straight into it as soon as you step over the threshold.

At our lowest, the week when we were *all* cranky, the week when the most beautiful full moon I've ever seen was clearly sticking its tongue out, I found myself stuck on a highway in a snowstorm trying to get to Mary. After more than an hour I was contemplating just turning around. It was all just too sucky. Time to go south. Or something.

For some reason I stayed in the snowstorm and made it to the hospice center. And as soon as I saw Mary's surprise at seeing me, all the crankiness dropped away. It was just me and Mary. Since I was the one who could, I chanted for both of us and then read to her from the well-known psychic Sylvia Brown's new book on mysteries because we both love sneaking peeks into past and future tense.

Because hospice situations can be intense, especially when the person you are visiting can only blink to communicate, there was no room for thinking about anything else but being present for Mary. When I left a short time later it felt like spring had arrived. The weather was still miserable, but my mood was light and I was happy and, of all things, relaxed for the first time in months.

Generosity grows joy. We see the good in ourselves, and we see it in other people. We watch a television show in which whole communities come out to build homes for families in desperate straits, and we are reminded, through the generosity depicted, that we have the capacity to take care of each other no matter who is president, no matter how cold it is, no matter how much trouble our own sweet mayor may find himself in before his term is over. Rock on.

THE SECOND INGREDIENT:
Extreme Ethics

The Buddhist Precepts

1. *Do not harm but cherish all life.*
2. *Do not take what is not given but respect the things of others.*
3. *Do not engage in sexual promiscuity but practice purity of mind and self-restraint.*
4. *Do not lie but speak the truth.*
5. *Do not partake in the production and transactions of firearms or chemical poisons which are injurious to public health and safety, nor of drugs and liquors which confuse or weaken the mind.*
6. *Do not waste but conserve energy and natural resources.*
7. *Do not harbor enmity against the wrongs of others but promote peace and justice through nonviolent means.*
8. *Do not cling to things that belong to you but practice generosity and the joy of sharing.*

The basic precepts are not passive. They can actively express a compassionate heart in our life. Not killing can grow into a reverence for life, a protective caring for all sentient beings who share life with us. Not stealing can become the basis for a wise ecology, honoring the limited resources of the earth and actively seeking ways to live and work that share our blessings worldwide. From this spirit can come a life of natural and healing simplicity. Out of not lying we can develop our voice to speak for compassion, understanding, and justice.

—Jack Kornfield, *A Path with Heart*

The first stop on my great pilgrimage west was to go east to visit my mother in West Springfield, Massachusetts. Without realizing it, I wanted her permission to move even farther away from her—a giant step of over two thousand miles. To my amazement, she brought the subject up first. We were sitting on my sister Sandy's deck. Above us, Blue Angels were practicing for an air show in a cobalt blue summer sky.

As we settled in for a long bout of catching up, Mom turned to me. "Go."

"What?"

"You need to put down roots. And you were happiest when you lived in Oregon."

She was right. I felt relieved, promising myself to start saving for a cross-country train ticket for her so she could visit at Christmas.

Since the conversation I had come for took all of three minutes, we had an entire day to talk about whatever surfaced in our minds.

It turned out to be ethics.

First we talked about parents of soldiers killed in Iraq and what we would do if a child of ours died. We agreed we'd do something akin to Cindy Sheehan. We wouldn't be quiet. Instead, we would try to come up with creative and legal ways to keep the war in front of people—to help it end as quickly as possible. Mom told me she was going to Washington soon to participate in a march for peace. Her anger at the current administration kept coming back to ethics—what she sees as a deep dishonesty. The absence of accountability for actions. The lack of transparency. I tried not to worry about her during the actual march. I wanted to believe that the D.C. police and counterprotesters wouldn't harm a white-haired great-grandmother.

Happily they didn't, so she is preparing for the next march.

While generosity is a strong ingredient, one ingredient does not make a cake. Generosity without the other ingredients can lead to a life of codependence, giving so much of ourselves away that there isn't anything left. It needs to be supported by the other ingredients, adventure and wisdom and clearheadedness, if it is to lead us into the land of everything is holy. Without the other ingredients we'll be too exhausted to look up from our futons.

Keeping a Clear Head

If we can get past laziness and fear, ethical behavior is deeply gratifying. A powerful ingredient, ethical behavior is inherent in everyone. If we can be ethical, anyone can be. Plus, anyone reading this book wants to be ethical. We especially want to be ethical going into a tough family situation, a work conflict, an argument with our partner. But how? How do we keep our heads in miserable situations that can potentially cause us, and the people around us, great harm? It helps to have someone who can give us advice. In the best-case scenario this would be someone who has been through at least a dozen of these situations and survived them all with grace. What does he or she have to tell us that might help?

One character who fits the bill of survivor extraordinaire can be found in the Flower Ornament Sutra, a massive compilation of good advice that appeared early in Mahayana Buddhist history. This character's name is Forest of Virtues. Because of his extraordinary knowledge—a small sample includes unobstructed knowledge, uninterrupted knowledge, knowledge without folly, and unerring knowledge—Forest is chock-full of advice about how to keep a clear head in any situation so that we can respond ethically to what is happening. He basically says that there are specific practices you can depend on, in addition to giving joy, whenever you find yourself confused. They are self-control, nonopposition, cultivating energy, nonconfusion about what is really going on, nonattachment, practicing what is difficult to do (just being quiet comes to mind here), and practicing truth. These practices protect our inherent wish to do what is right no matter what is going on around us.

Self-Control

Self-control can be a lifelong practice. Most of us never get it down completely. I know, for example, that the day I stop cursing is the day of my last breath. I remain too thrilled by the sound of curses coming out of my own boarding-school-trained-debutante-ized lips to let go completely in this lifetime. If nothing else, the habit keeps me humble and hesitant to judge anyone else who is wrestling with stinking habits.

It is worth struggling with, however, because I know how deeply comforting it is to be around someone who has self-control, particularly in situations where we aren't sure of our own: the one who doesn't drink, who says no to drugs, who shrugs off a potential affair with an "I'm complimented, but I just couldn't do that to my partner." Sunryu Suzuki was a wonderful, handsome, Japanese Zen teacher who was a member of the first generation of Asian teachers to take on significant numbers of Western students. Suzuki did this in San Francisco, during the era of free love. Urban myth has it that plenty of his students had crushes on him. Some were pretty aggressive, hiding in his bed at night, waiting for him to find them.

As far as I can tell, he kindly refused all opportunities. In one interview, when a beloved student told him that she didn't know if she had the willpower to stay clear of sexual relations with him, he told her not to worry—he had enough willpower for them both.

There is a bone-deep safety in this behavior. It helps you to relax into looking for an ethical way out of a tough situation without being clouded by a lack of self-control.

Nonopposition

Forest's advice about nonopposition hit me by surprise at first. Difficult situations have at their epicenter opposition, don't they? But then I remembered a class I was sent to back when I lived in

the world as a management consultant. It was a class on negotia-
tion. The title was "Getting to Yes." I expected the trainers to teach
us to always sit on the same side of the table with the person we
were negotiating with as a demonstration of nonopposition. What
I didn't expect was to learn that it didn't make sense to even start
negotiating anything until I had proven to my "opponent" that I
had heard exactly what he had been saying during our initial interactions. This proved to be excruciatingly hard work, not to mention
humiliating. The whole first day I was so off in my paraphrasing
that it was as though I came from a completely different planet.
I felt slightly better when my partner did an equally lousy job
paraphrasing what I said. It hit me that we all could use a refresher
course on listening. Especially those of us (me!) who think we
listen well.

It took the entire first day of the class for us to finally hear
each other. The biggest surprise of the class was this: By the time I
finally got a positive head nod from my opponent that I had actually heard what was being said, we were both determined to find a
win-win solution. We not only understood the other person's point
of view, each of us understood how we got there, and out of that
understanding had grown empathy—and friendship. We spent the
next twenty-four hours hunting for a solution. Over beers. Into the
night. Jogging the next morning. It was that important.

That exercise convinced me that there is always a solution to
conflict that both sides can live with—even when we are represent-
ing different parts of Ireland.

Cultivating Energy

Putting energy into ethical behavior gives it the fuel it needs to keep burning. In the sutra, Forest offers us a list of the kinds of energy he means. The list is long. It includes great energy, excellent energy, outstanding energy, exalted energy, and comprehensive energy, among others. He teaches that when we are filled with these sorts of energy we naturally become freed from greed, hatred, delusion, pride, and conceit.

Watching a young friend of mine, Jake, put energy into training for the Detroit Marathon, I remembered how true that was for me back in my running and skiing days. I took up cross-country skiing in my thirties. It was hard. I was slow. At the time, I was in love with a cross-country skiing connoisseur, someone who made it look as easy as microwaving a Stouffer's pizza, so easy that it never occurred to me to ask for instructions. I figured I'd eventually learn how to walk faster on the skis.

To demonstrate my commitment to our love, one weekend I agreed to drive to Traverse City, Michigan, to cheer him on as he skied the Vasa, a cross-country skiing marathon. Somehow I had agreed to ski it as well. I vaguely remember thinking that the worst thing that could possibly happen would be that I would learn how to ski faster.

Instead, from the sound of the starter's gun I was the last person in the race. At every hill I fell farther and farther behind since I had no idea how to get up the hills. My solution was to take off the skis, walk up the hills, put the skis back on, and keep going.

Halfway through the race a park ranger sidled up to me to ask me if I could ski any faster. At the rate I was going I wouldn't make it back before nightfall. I nodded that I could and from that moment gave the race all the energy I had. Everything else simply dropped away. The only sound was the sound of the skis and my breathing. World War III could have been happening right beside me and I wouldn't have noticed. There simply wasn't any room in my brain for anything but finishing the race. No room for emotions. Not even room for wondering what had possessed me to say yes. Only effort and increasingly ragged breath.

Later the same ranger asked me if he could give me a lift in. He said not to worry about anyone seeing me, that most people had left. It took a lot to say no, but I did. Making it to the finish line just as the sun was starting to set, I came in about an hour after the second-to-last person in the race. As difficult as it was, to this day I am grateful that I didn't stop before I was finished. On that day all I felt was a sense of relief and general goodwill. No greed, no anger, no pride, no humiliation. A sweet diffused happiness.

Nonconfusion

Forest could have stopped with energy, I think. But these enlightening beings are as bad as TV actor Tony Shalhoub's obsessive-compulsive detective, Monk—they have to make sure all the details are covered. After energy, Forest addresses nonconfusion. My first clues about what the heck he meant came from my friend Haju Linda Murray. I lived with Haju for a year in the Ann Arbor Zen Buddhist

Temple. There I was able to see how she was raising her two young daughters. One of the things that struck me was that whenever there was a problem, Haju would gather data and then not do anything for a while. Sometimes it would drive me nuts because it would seem so obvious that the kids needed a scolding or that a visit to a teacher was called for. But Haju waited. And when she responded to the situation I was often struck by how wise her response was. For example, when her older daughter was fifteen she fell in love with the boy next door. We all had opinions about this. Most of us advised Haju (not that she had asked for opinions) to keep the teens separate, to keep her daughter busy, maybe to send her away.

Haju listened to all of us. And then, after a few days of no response, she simply made the young man a part of the family. The two teens had a safe, touching love affair for several years before moving back into separate lives. The families remain close friends, no babies were made, and we all lived happily ever after thanks to Haju's quiet wisdom.

• • •

On a pilgrimage in Korea in 1999, I had the pleasure of meeting a Zen master who was the spitting image of Charlie Brown in oversized glasses. Iltal Sunim had lots of advice about being ethical, but the main thing I remember him saying was that mindfulness matters the most when it comes to staying clear of confusion. Stay in the moment. Pay attention to what matters. Ignore everything else. That's it. Maybe he said more, but that is all the translator told me. It is impossible to be confused when we are fully mindful.

There is a hilarious story about Buddha teaching his attendant, Ananda, about mindfulness and the importance of waiting for the correct reaction to surface. The two are walking through a forest on a hot summer day when Buddha turns to Ananda and asks him to go back to a river they crossed some miles back to get some water to drink. Ananda trudges back, but when he gets there some carts have just crossed the river, making it muddy. Ananda walks back to Buddha empty-handed. When he reaches him Ananda tells Buddha that they need to wait a little longer. He has heard that there is a river a couple of miles ahead of them; he will get water there and bring it back.

Buddha's reaction? He tells Ananda to go back to the first river. If the water is still dirty, Ananda is to sit on its banks and watch. Sooner or later the water will clear. Sure enough, when Ananda goes back the river is almost clear. He watches it clear completely and then gets some water. By the time he makes it back to Buddha he understands the value of waiting mindfully until the correct response to a situation becomes obvious.

Nonattachment

The thing about these behaviors is that they build on each other, and they build momentum. It is pretty easy, when we first commit to a spiritual path, to get caught up in how wonderful we are since our lives shift, sometimes dramatically. Forest warns us not to get attached to anything since in the end, all of these behaviors are aimed at one end: ethical behavior.

Nonattachment may be the most difficult advice to swallow here given our innate Velcro nature. Nonattachment is about not taking things personally, starting with our own karma. A Jesuit friend of mine tells me that it takes more than ten years of training in his spiritual tradition to get to indifference, the Jesuit form of nonattachment. I believe him.

It helps to have a model to see what Forest is trying to say. If we watch, someone will show us how this works. For me that person is an American Theravadan nun who travels the world depending completely on the kindness of strangers for her survival. A few years ago we were driving in a car from Detroit to Ann Arbor together, and I asked her if everywhere was her home.

"Yes."

This sense of being at home anywhere, with anyone filling in the role of family, can be deeply comforting when we find ourselves swimming, rudder free, across the ocean we call life. Watching for the goodness in people makes it easier to spot, and relaxing anywhere makes it easier to be kind and helpful.

Practicing What Is Difficult

When our man Forest introduces the concept of "that which is difficult to attain," he is talking about never giving up. Think about Lance Armstrong. Or my friend Deb O'Brien, who faces debilitating diseases at every turn and still keeps getting up in the morning. Jerry Lewis and his telethons. Ellen DeGeneres and her dancing. These people are in it for the long haul, however long that haul becomes.

Practicing Truth

As Forest winds down, he reminds us that there is always something we can do to be helpful in a situation. If we pay attention
carefully, what that something is will be Day-Glo clear. Maybe it is
taking a baby to hold from an exhausted parent. Maybe it is washing piles of dishes at a friend's house or talking to the uncle whom
nobody can stand because he can't sit still without a Cuban cigar in
his mouth. Maybe we can simply listen to people talk about their
worries. Watching for that right action can be fun—sort of like a
three-dimensional computer game. We discover that even small
gestures can improve the overall energy of a room.

All these teachings lead up to the practice of truth. This is
where small-*e* ethics become big-*e* Ethics. It helps to believe in
karma. When we can be honest in the world, it responds in kind.
According to many religious traditions, karma is a law. When we
start to really pay attention to our lives, we can watch it play out in
a thousand different ways. When I was raising my son, Sarth, I was
drowning in the obligations of single parenting and a demanding
job. That meant that our interactions, starting from when he was
about nine years old, grew shorter and shorter. I loved him completely, still do. But I didn't have time to play, to hang out, to see
how he was surviving his preteen and later teen years.

When he was headed for trouble I didn't see it, and when I
finally pulled my head out of the sand of too many obligations, we
were two aliens staring at each other across an ocean of hurt and

addiction. That he is still alive today is a measure of his resilience as a human being. He should be dead. It has taken the better part of ten years to begin to get back the playfulness and the sheer hilarity of our early years together. Karma.

Raising my daughter, who is ten years younger than Sarth, I worked hard to be more available. I swear I chewed a million holes in both cheeks when impatience made me want to cut her off in the middle of a conversation. It wasn't that I didn't love her; I adore her. It was that a multitude of demands had turned me into a time-efficiency, multitasking ogre. By being excruciatingly mindful of my tendencies, I was able to be available to her through most of her trials and tribulations and to be a bit of a friend to her friends in the way my mother had been available to me and mine. I can do better, but at least as of this writing she hasn't had to face the addiction demons her brother did.

The thing about karma is that nobody can play it out for us. Truth is truth. Things are what they are. We can't give it away, sell it, bribe someone to take ours on. Even the Buddha said, "I have every kind of medicine to help people no matter what their problem is, but I can't make them take it." This teaching grew out of a situation in which one of his followers, foreseeing a war that would destroy many of the people who lived in the kingdom where most of Buddha's extended family lived, rushed to Buddha to ask him if he could stop the war.

"I can't."

"Why not?"

"You can't make merited karma disappear."

This is the tattoo I want on my left wrist so I can see it each day. Everything we do matters. Everything. Oh, how I wish it weren't so, given the truck-driving mouth I have, but there it is.

The trick, then, is to take Forest's advice—to be generous and controlled; to let go of our penchant for arguing just because we love it so; to be clearheaded and energetic and as free from attachment to an outcome as we can be. These things foster truth. And promote positive karma. We need to pay attention to what our senses are telling us all the time—our seeing, hearing, smelling, tasting, touching—so we can catch ourselves before we cause problems, any problems. When we do, we save the world, an action at a time.

It is tough to live a life of truth. It is really hard to pay close enough attention to what is going on around us to even know what the truth of each situation is. But when we don't, the consequences can be serious. Last year Abby, a good friend of mine, decided to commit suicide. Since she had tried several times before, those of us who know and love her had learned to pay attention to cries for help, whatever the form.

The most recent cry came in the form of a garbled phone call from a local hotel. Happily, the person she called knew her history and that there was no reason that Abby would be staying in a hotel fifteen miles away from her own house if she wasn't planning to hurt herself. Sure enough, the overdose almost worked. After a painful visit to the local hospital's emergency room, Abby decided enough was enough and signed herself into a three-month-long intensive psychiatric program nearby.

The first time I went to visit her she looked terrible. Gaunt. Gray. Tired. This is a woman who is usually the life of any party, whether there is a party or not. She is funny and beautiful and can sing the bark right off a tree.

I was so caught off balance by how she looked that I started blathering away about pretty meaningless stuff—television reality shows, weather, traffic. She didn't respond at all. Looked at me a little. Didn't say a word.

After about twenty minutes I had wound down enough to ask her if there was anything I could do to help her.

"Well, it is so noisy here. People keep talking at me."

Oops.

If I had been paying attention I would have seen, two minutes into my blathering, that she didn't want to talk. She also didn't want to be talked to.

So I shut the hell up. After a while I just started chanting a little between pauses of silence. The energy in the room changed. A small smile appeared. She told me I could come back to visit her.

Today Abby is back entertaining all of us with her energy and forthrightness about every little thing. I still cringe when I remember how I harmed her needlessly because I didn't look or listen when I knew better.

The Resistance Ogres

Even with the motivation provided by numberless hells, each one utterly related to the family of screwups of a lifetime, it is tough to be ethical, to do what is right, in an era that doesn't seem to reward it. Five types of resistances get in our way: our attachment to sensual desire, ill will, laziness, restlessness or worry, and uncertainty about our own capacity to deal with a particular situation.

1. Desire

We all have desires. If we didn't feed some of them, starvation would have cleaned us all off a childless planet. The issue here isn't desire in and of itself. The problem is our attachment. We're greedy. It is in our nature to want more food, sex, drink, television, money. A recent landmark study by the Substance Abuse and Mental Health Services Administration reported, for example, that 23 percent of Americans had been on a recent drinking binge, which they defined as more than five drinks in one sitting. Almost a quarter of us had binged. If it wasn't you and it wasn't me, it was one of our best friends, a sibling, our kid, or a parent. One in ten of us smoked marijuana in the past year. Over 14.5 million people had used it in the thirty days prior to the survey. Another 2.3 million of us had used sufficient cocaine to make us stupid enough to forget our ethics. In Detroit we lived with the destruction of all three drugs every day. Abandoned kids, homes, partners, pets. Petty crime all the time. Violence. Suicide. All growing out of runaway desire.

2. *Ill Will*

It is also hard to be ethical when we are angry. Who doesn't get angry? Even saints get angry sometimes. At least all the ones I know, and I know quite a few. The problem is what happens when we cling to the anger. Anger blocks all sorts of information headed in our direction that could help alleviate a difficult situation. Instead, we see red. As you know, this is literally true. And it doesn't take much for that anger to morph into revenge if we feel we've been wronged. This is insanity. Revenge never fixed anything. When Buddha's son, Rahula, wanted to become a monk, Buddha offered him revolutionary advice. He told him to "be like the earth." We can urinate, defecate, vomit, weep, and bleed on the earth without fear of its revenge. In its history it hasn't retaliated. Instead, it simply cleans up after us as best it can. To my knowledge, the earth never hits back, never plots to get even with us, even when we deserve it. In terms of anger and ill will, we need to "be like the earth."

3. *Laziness*

Sometimes we are too lazy to be ethical. We could call that person or e-mail her. We could write a letter, make a phone call. But we don't. It's not like others don't notice. They do. I'm pretty sure that my mother was the last United States citizen to admit out loud that George W. Bush had won a second term in office. Long after the presidential election was over, she was down in Ohio protesting the count—a noble effort on her part. When she finally went home to Massachusetts, there was a letter waiting for her from Howard Dean. It was asking for her political support in his campaign to become the chair of the Democratic National Committee.

Her response?

I'll just say that she was not happy at all.

She was unhappy, not because she disagrees with his politics. She doesn't. And she likes it that he can be outraged. She was mad because of what she saw as his laziness. "He should have been in Ohio fighting for votes. He was lazy." I'm guessing that many people agreed with her, even though he won the position. A quick visit of support would have gone a long way with loyal Democrats.

4. *Worry*

Worry also gets in our way. I can remember working with a chief financial officer of a fast-growing high-tech company who, in confidence, told me story after story of unethical behavior on the part of the company's owners. They weren't breaking any laws exactly, they were just unethical. At one point I asked her why she didn't do anything about what she saw. She had all the data. Her response was that she was worried she would lose her job. I did everything I could think of to convince her that sooner or later unethical companies go under and everyone loses her job. Karma is karma. She ignored me even as the company went under and everyone lost their jobs.

5. *Not Trusting Ourselves*

Not trusting ourselves is the final hindrance. This is why the prework of having faith in ourselves matters so much. We need to trust our gut reactions to situations. Now that I have been living on this planet for a half century I am convinced—utterly—that each of us knows what is the right thing to do in any situation. What stops us is our penchant for second-guessing ourselves. Fear feeds the second-guessing. What is so sad about this is that when I sit with people as they lie dying they *always* regret the times when they didn't do the right thing. And they always know exactly what it was they could have done. They remember the specific moments and relive them, feeling deep regret over and over. The third time I sat with someone who had this experience I vowed to always do the right thing even if I looked back at a situation to see that I could have been more skillful. I'll have enough things to be sorry about without this form of regret as well.

In the Zen tradition there is a wonderful story about an old Zen master, Huang Po, who was walking with a man who, when they came to a river, walked right across the top of the water. Huang said that the man's act was completely unnecessary. In life we have physical bodies. They don't need to be special. We don't need to be special. Obstacles appear to slow us down. Okay, then, we're slowed down. There isn't anything inherently good or bad about this. We don't need to waste time judging things that don't matter or trying to be special. We only need to trust our reactions to the situations we find ourselves in without getting caught in superficialities. Soeng Hyang tells a great story about this. Her teacher, Zen master Seung Sahn, had been in the United States for about six months when someone asked him if there were any women Zen masters in Korea. His response was no, that women "can't get enlightenment."

Soeng Hyang, a woman, just looked at him, shocked. Even after that short a period he was known for his wonderful dharma talks in which he advised spiritual seekers, "Don't make man, don't make woman, don't make anything." So she asked him what he meant by saying that women couldn't get enlightenment.

His response was to look at her: "So, you're a woman."

She needed to get past the label.

These labels catch us coming and going. Its helpful to get under them, to simply live our lives. This is where the deepest ethical behavior becomes available to us, the compassion and wisdom that we are so hungry to tap in to. We need to sit up straight, eat our Wheaties, and do what we can to be helpful to the world, even if this is measured in one phone call a month or our five-dollar donation to the local Sierra Club chapter or hurricane or earthquake relief.

• • •

As we learn to rely on Forest's advice and to dodge our resistances as best we can, we naturally become more ethical. We take responsibility for each other. Theodore Roosevelt once wrote in a letter to his daughter Alice, "Remember that when you do foolish things, you make it certain that worse than foolish things will be ascribed to you." The same is true for acts of wisdom.

These days my heroes are the whistle-blowers, those people who have the courage to trust themselves enough to call out huge institutions. Happily, I am not alone. Three years ago *Time* magazine named three whistle-blowers as persons of the year: Cynthia Cooper at WorldCom, Coleen Rowley from the FBI, and Enron's Sherron Watkins. That the mainstream press honored specific behavior instead of a person tells me how desperate we've become for clear-cut ethical actions. WorldCom's vice president of internal audit, Cynthia Cooper, didn't expect her life to be turned upside down when she told the company's board audit committee that the company had been using accounting practices that were "suspect." But it was.

Like most whistle-blowers I have known or read about, Cynthia Cooper didn't start out as one. Apparently in March 2002 she was told by another executive that WorldCom's corporate accounting department had taken $400 million out of the company's reserves to boost its income. When she went to the accountants they told her it was not her problem. Except that it was. Cooper didn't back down even when the company's chief financial officer, instead of praising her for doing her job, told her to back off.

Fortunately, she didn't. By double-checking the accounting work, she found billions of dollars categorized incorrectly. The accountants had cooked the books so that a $662 million loss appeared to be a $2.4 billion profit. As a result of her report to the board, she received no kudos; instead, friends abandoned her and the press hounded her while thousands of people in Clinton, Mississippi, lost their jobs. She was lucky that the board backed her behavior, ultimately firing her boss. In the end WorldCom admitted that profits had been inflated by $9 billion. A historical

untruth. The largest accounting fraud in the history of this country, at least that we know of. Today WorldCom is MCI. It is doing
okay, I guess. Rumor has it that Cooper never received any thanks
for her efforts from her colleagues. It is hard not to think about
how many schools in Detroit could be keeping their lights on with
the money WorldCom spent sorting out all the accounting irregu-
larities. Or how many jobs might still exist in Clinton.

Cynthia has been very public about her reaction to the whole
experience. Depression. Lost weight. Shed hair. And even though
she tells people she would do it again, "Doing the right thing
regardless of the costs" takes a deep trust in oneself.

While Cynthia Cooper still works for MCI as I write this, the
case of Sherron Watkins played out in a much different way. When
she stood up to Enron she was demoted "thirty-three floors from
her mahogany executive suite to a 'skanky office' with a rickety
metal desk and a pile of make-work projects" until she simply gave
up and left. Watkins was the vice president of corporate development in August 2001 when she sent a memo to Enron's chairman,
Kenneth Lay, registering her concern about the accounting practices in the company. She was genuinely afraid that Enron would
face scandals if they continued to use off-the-books partnerships to
hide company losses.

Lay got Enron's lawyer to take a look. The response was
that there were no major problems. In the meantime Enron's chief
financial officer, Andrew Fastow, responded to her concerns by trying to fire her. By November 2001 Enron had filed for bankruptcy,

after publicly admitting that since 1997 it had overstated profits—by some $600 million. Thousands of people's lives were deeply harmed as Enron fell, taking reputations and livelihoods with it.

For Coleen Rowley, the crisis was September 11, 2001. Leading up to that day, a man named Zacarias Moussaoui had paid cash to take a flight simulation course for a Boeing 747. When it became clear to his instructor that Moussaoui was incapable of taking off or landing a plane after more than fifty hours of instruction, the teacher went to the Federal Bureau of Investigation to register his concerns about his student. At the time Rowley was the attorney for the FBI's Minneapolis office. When her office looked into Moussaoui's background they found evidence that the French intelligence was concerned about probable links between Moussaoui and Islamic extremist groups.

Based on this research, Rowley sent a request to FBI headquarters asking for a warrant to search the man's computer and personal effects.

She was turned down. That July an FBI agent in Phoenix also wrote a memo that reflected deep concerns about the number of Middle Eastern men attending U.S. flight schools. Nothing happened with those concerns either.

Here is how Rowley responded in her famous whistleblowing memo:

> *The fact is that key FBI HQ personnel whose job it was to assist and coordinate with field division agents on terrorism investigations and the obtaining and use of ... searches (and who*

*theoretically were privy to many more sources of intelligence
information than field division agents) continued to, almost
inexplicably, throw up roadblocks and undermine Minneapolis' by-now desperate efforts to obtain a ... search warrant,
long after the French intelligence service provided its information and probable cause became clear. HQ personnel brought
up almost ridiculous questions in their apparent efforts to
undermine the probable cause. In all of their conversations
and correspondence, HQ personnel never disclosed to the Minneapolis agents that the Phoenix Division had, only approximately three weeks earlier, warned of Al Qaeda operatives in
flight schools seeking flight training for terrorist purposes!*

You know the next part of the story. On September 11, 2001,
two commercial jet planes were hijacked and flown into the World
Trade Center in New York City. Another was hijacked and flown
into the Pentagon. A fourth plane was also hijacked but crashed
before its mission was completed.

On that day the world changed. Terrorists proved their ability to shut down the economy of the most powerful nation in the
world. Years later we are still not completely back on our feet.

To add to the heartbreak, a subsequent search of Moussaoui's
computer yielded information that could have prevented the crisis.
Moreover, according to Rowley, "Certain facts have been omitted,
downplayed, glossed over and/or mischaracterized in an effort to
avoid or minimize personal and/or institutional embarrassment."

As painful as her words were, and still are, her honesty is the
honesty that we need to grow in ourselves to mature spiritually. We

need to trust our own guts, and then, not with the intention of harming anyone or any institution, have the courage to say what we see. Out loud. Even if we are the only one. Maybe there won't be any changes as a result of our efforts. Or maybe the whole world will change.

What if you find yourself in a situation where you just can't get clear? Mantras help. There are mantras in every spiritual tradition. Call on Jesus or Mary or Muhammad or Buddha for help. Simply asking will shift your energy. "Please help me to see clearly." Ask and give yourself the gift of quiet. Then ask again. Repeat until you see what you need to do. I'm told that any mantra works, even "They're all worms." Feel free to make up your own.

What if you feel called to whistle-blow but don't know where to start? Stay close to home and just watch. Or pick up a phone to report a simple problem that keeps recurring. In Detroit this can range from trash that hasn't been collected to darkened streetlights to abandoned cars. One week a friend tried to call the city to ask them to swing by a second time to pick up the trash they had ignored, and after almost ten minutes of followed recorded instructions and pushing buttons, he finally made it through to the city's customer service line. There he was informed that, although he had reached the customer service hotline, it was full. Click. Just as we started to talk about calling a local television news station's problem-solving team, a garbage truck showed up at the front of the abbey, proving to us that even the slightest effort can be rewarded.

three

THE THIRD INGREDIENT:
Tolerance

Above all remember ... that you have a great opportunity.... Millions all over the world would give almost anything they possess to be where you are. You are there by no desert or merit of your own, but only by lucky chance.

Deserve it then. Study, do your work. Be honest, frank, fearless and get some grasp of the real values of life. You will meet, of course, curious little annoyances....

—W. E. B. DuBois

To move to the Northwest, I decided to drive across the country in my trustee old Subaru, or TOS for short. Even after 100,000 miles it had never let me down. No flat tires. No radiator leaks. No check-engine lights blinking in the night. Crossing the plains of the Midwest into the mountains of the great West would be a breeze in what promised to be a mild autumn.

This meant that I did my best not to see the flat tire when I came out of a breakfast diner at 7:00 a.m. somewhere between

Mitchell and Chamberlain, South Dakota. Mostly I tried not to think about the three hours I had just driven in the dark to try to get a head start through the long, mostly flat state.

I was standing in the middle of a driveway surrounded on two sides by plains. A person could see at least five miles in each direction. Not a house or a building in sight. The diner was on the third side and the highway on the fourth. Beside the diner, though, was a garage, and in that garage was a plaid-shirted, cowboy boot–wearing teenager working on a red Ford pickup truck. Walking over, doing my best not to panic, I told him about my tire. He nodded and walked over to see for himself.

Could he help? He sized me up, nodded again, and walked into the garage for some tools. When I asked him if I could watch him work, another nod. I chatted feverishly while he took the tire off, patched it, and put it back on the car. He probably didn't care at all about anything I was talking about.

He was done in an hour. At the end of it he would only take twenty dollars from me, said, "It'll be okay," and went back to fixing his truck. Watching him, I was struck by how tolerant he was with my panicked state. I want to be him. I want to be able to do my work quietly while some nutso woman runs off at the mouth in my direction at 7:30 in the morning. I want to tell her it will be okay without needing to lecture her or solve her problems or tell her to please shut the hell up.

. . .

Generosity, once you start, becomes its own habit. Ethics is the same. In my experience, the more generous and ethical we are, the more of both we become. These two ingredients lead us to the third one: tolerance. Maybe it is because, as hokey as this sounds, our hearts are opening up enough to allow tolerance in. In any event, generosity makes us feel good about ourselves. Ethical behavior makes us feel capable and strong. They build on each other and help us see when someone else is being generous or ethical. (There is always someone else, I promise.) We appreciate more, and we are able to accept more of the sorrow in our lives precisely because we are experiencing more joy. A sense of holiness can pop up unexpectedly and then start to settle into our experience of people, places, and events.

With that sense comes more tolerance. Detroit taught me how good it feels to be genuinely tolerant. The person who taught me the most was Eugene.

Almost five feet tall, he might be in his forties. It is hard to tell. The man is shaped like a fire hydrant. I always wondered what people meant when they described someone that way, and then I met Eugene. His little head has a tuft of hair that is partly gray, always greasy, never combed. His eyes bulge out of his head. They are crossed. Usually his nose is running. Sometimes he is drooling.

Eugene has a pot belly that is always exposed, even when the temperature drop below zero. His clothes are filthy when they aren't brand new. Sometimes his shoes don't match, and it is hard to understand him because he talks with a lisp and has a partially fixed harelip.

I'm guessing that most people think his I.Q. is low because he speaks slowly and his words are garbled. It isn't. Eugene is wily, funny, and vicious.

Most people think he is homeless. He isn't homeless either; he just looks like he is.

Eugene started showing up at Still Point's door about six months after we moved into the building. First he asked for money. Since we don't give people money—it's the law of the street—we gave him empty soda pop cans he could turn in. When we ran out of cans we gave him bananas. Then he started to come to the door asking for bananas and water. We gave him the fruit but after a while said that he had to go home for the water since Ango followed him one day and saw that he lived only a couple of blocks away.

Eugene started asking for other things. Aspirin. The bathroom. Suitcases. On the days when he came to the door and we didn't give him what he wanted, he would throw a tantrum. He'd curse at the top of his lungs and march down the steps looking for something to throw or hit. One time he was so mad at me that he opened my gas tank and was looking for something to put into it when I interrupted him. Running away, he was still cursing me.

We gave Eugene clothes. Sweaters, sweatshirts, sneakers, gym pants. One time he showed up at the front door during a Sunday meditation service demanding to see me. When I got to him, he had stripped down to a T-shirt and sweatpants. The pants looked like they were falling off. His whole butt was hanging out of the back of them. He looked at me: "I can't unknot the string, and I have to piss." Even wedging a screwdriver into the knot wouldn't unravel it. Finally we cut the string and found him different pants.

Right about then his requests doubled. At first he was at the door four times a day, then five, always with a story about why he needed immediate help. He's a good teacher, we told ourselves. He's forcing us to see our own impatience.

Yeah, right.

He started showing up before dawn and once or twice late at night. And if nobody answered the doorbell, he'd lean on it for a while and then start pounding on the front window with all his might. And while it is easy to spout sweet little sayings about how we should respect each other, living with Eugene showed us all how thin that veneer can be.

Following several months of pounding and tantrums, Ango finally sat Eugene down and gave him a formal set of rules:

STILL POINT RULES FOR EUGENE

1. Only ring the doorbell twice. NO KNOCKING ON DOOR. If door is not answered after 2 bell rings, we are not available. Come back another time.

2. DO NOT YELL at anyone who answers the door or who is out in front of the house. Please try to be kind, Eugene.

3. There will be no money given to Eugene at any time by anyone who answers the door.

4. Eugene is welcome to have any pop bottles. Also an occasional banana, orange, or cookie/sweet.

5. Only come to this house ONCE A DAY. One day at a time, Eugene!

TIME RESTRICTIONS

WE ARE CLOSED ON MONDAY. Please do not come for bottles on this day until after 10:00 a.m.

Tuesday–Saturday: 7–11 a.m. or 1:30–5:00 p.m.

DO NOT COME BETWEEN 12:00 NOON AND 1:00 p.m.!!!!

Sunday: DO NOT COME UNTIL AFTER 2:00 p.m.!!!!!

We are happy to help you with bottles and a little bit of food, Eugene. We care about you. However ... it is important that you follow these rules in order to continue visiting us. If you are not able to follow these rules, then you may be asked not to come to our house anymore.

He was able to follow the rules for about a week. On a day when he had made several visits, mostly between noon and one, I was painting in the basement when I heard his all-too-familiar pounding on the front window. I'd already given him cans, bananas, and water. When it became clear that he was not going to stop, I lost it. Rushing upstairs, furious, I opened the door and yelled at him, "That's it, Eugene! I'm calling the police!"

We both knew the police had better things to do than chase him away. Even so, Eugene ran down the sidewalk, crying, "I'm sorry, I'm sorry!" and I felt like the Wicked Witch of the West. After that he became the Eugene Sutra. We could all see exactly where our tolerance was cracking and how we could handle anything he came up with as long as we'd had at least six hours of sleep and at least one round of meditation sitting behind us.

We've learned that the rules for Eugene had to keep changing because his situation kept changing—that black-and-white policies don't work in a world where impermanence is the rule of the day. In the meantime, word got out on the street that we saved cans for him. We found black plastic bags full of them on the front porch. Eugene taught us about tolerance and patience and restraint with every ring of the doorbell.

On the toughest days I learned to lean heavily on the Metta Sutra or Sutra on Loving-Kindness. Just when I would be ready to yell, I'd start reciting it softly to myself:

This is what should be done
By one who is skilled in goodness,
And who knows the path of peace:
Let them be able and upright,
Straightforward and gentle in speech.
Humble and not conceited,
Contented and easily satisfied.
Unburdened with duties and frugal in their ways.
Peaceful and calm, and wise and skillful,
Not proud and demanding in nature.
Let them not do the slightest thing
That the wise would later reprove.
Wishing: in gladness and in safety,
May all beings be at ease!
Whatever living beings there may be;

Whether they are weak or strong, omitting none,

The great or the mighty, medium, short, or small.

The seen and the unseen,

Those living near and far away,

Those born and to-be-born—

May all beings be at ease!

Let none deceive another,

Or despise any being in any state,

Let none through anger or ill will

Wish harm upon another.

Even as a mother protects with her life

Her child, her only child,

So with a boundless heart

Should one cherish all living beings;

Radiating kindness over the entire world:

Spreading upwards to the skies,

And downwards to the depths;

Outward and unbounded,

Freed from hatred and ill will.

Whether standing or walking, seated or lying down

Free from drowsiness,

One should sustain this recollection.

Eugene would look at me and smile. He was happy for company, even yelling company. After a while we all realized that, more
than anything else, he was lonely. When one of the residents took

time to visit with him on the porch, even for as little as ten minutes, the rate of doorbell ringing decreased significantly. When he moved away, we missed him. Happily, a character named Calvin took his place, showing up almost daily for a sandwich and some juice.

Faith in Ourselves Redux

Genuine tolerance means accepting what is happening to us without feeling obligated to react with blame, anger, or hate. It is incredibly hard work. In his wonderful book *When Jesus Came to Harvard*, Harvey Cox reports that the virtue the thousands of students he taught at Harvard most valued was tolerance: "They were living examples of the old Native American adage, 'Never judge a man until you have walked a mile in his moccasins,' which implies, of course, that after that mile you will not want to judge him at all" (p. 9).

It is an easy yes when someone asks us if we believe we are, or should be, tolerant. But without patience we can't get to tolerance. And without trusting ourselves to have the capacity to be tolerant, we can't get there either.

When we trust ourselves, that trust opens up a space for tolerance for ourselves and others. As quirky as we are—and we're all pretty quirky—you will find you don't need anyone else's approval for how you live your life. You aren't dependent on anyone else's opinion of your clothes, hair, weight, demeanor. In return, you are less judgmental of everyone else. Your capacity to simply accept everyone as they are grows. As a result, you get less caught up in judgment and are more open to appreciation. Compassion grows out of that appreciation and with it a sense of endearment for whomever you are interacting with.

I have watched my friend Janet trust herself more and more. When she first started meditating she was a pretty, quiet school teacher—maybe forty. In one year her mother died and her father's mental state deteriorated so dramatically that she sold her house to live with him. For a while I watched her take orders from the rest of her family—how her father needed to be cared for, what kind of a job made the most sense for her. Then suddenly it seemed she had discarded her concern regarding other people's opinions of her. I chocked it up to her spiritual practice. She had been doing lots of retreats, had been meditating, had been showing up at the temple, first to volunteer and then to live there for a while. Within a couple of months she quit her job to train for a career path that made more sense to her, even though it would mean a dramatic decrease in annual income. She cut her hair, changed her style of clothes, grew so much spiritually that you could feel her sweet energy even before she walked into a room. When you are around her you know that no matter who you are, she is not going to judge you or your behavior. She will only look for ways to be helpful in a situation. And when there is something that needs doing, she does it. She trusts herself to know her limits.

Leaning In

A good way to know whether we really trust ourselves is to be thrown into situations where we have no choice. In the retreat with

Soeng Hyang where I was humbled by her question about greeting a Zen master in the road, she asked me during an interview if
I would do the one dharma talk of the retreat. Following a long,
jagged inhale of breath, "Of course." In that moment I knew what
the subject would be: how I manage to stay to the ends of retreats
without running away.

Even after years of attending or leading long retreats, there is
always a moment when most of me says, "This so sucks. I'm gone."
By now I know the phenomenon is the result of physical and emo-
tional exhaustion and is a sign that the retreat is working its magic,
although it doesn't feel like it at the time. And every time I hear
myself saying the escape words out loud, I know to kick in three
antidotes: to lean in to the retreat harder; to relax and trust that I'm
doing the best I can (and so is everybody else); and to remember
words of encouragement from a monk or nun who has lived the
spiritual path before me.

Leaning in means looking at what I'm resisting and, instead
of being lazy or trying to escape, putting more energy into everything. Here are two examples from that retreat.

Right before I left Detroit for the airport, I fell hard on my
left knee. I knew a sore knee meant that sitting in meditation would
be agony by midmorning. We had the option of sitting on chairs. I
also knew that if I sat on a chair I would certainly fall asleep. So I
sat on a cushion in a half lotus. And when I couldn't practice for the
pain, I stood behind my cushion along with beginners who weren't
used to long sittings. And stayed.

Leaning in example number two: When I went on pilgrimage with my root teacher, Samu Sunim, to Korea in 1999, we ate seaweed soup more than frequently. Soon I was afraid even to look at what we were given to eat. Leaving Korea, I promised myself that I would never have to eat a seaweed-based soup again, healthy benefits be damned. At that same retreat some years later, lunch was brought out and I could smell the soup before it reached the room: seaweed. Instant nausea, a cramped stomach. When the server came around to me, however, I stuck my empty bowl out as far as I could, asking for a big serving. If we were going to eat seaweed soup, I was going to eat it with gusto. The great surprise? It was delicious.

Outside of retreats, leaning in can mean sticking with a bookkeeping problem until it is solved or staying on the phone with a colleague who needs a witness to his heartbreak even though there at least five other things you would rather be doing. Leaning in is a lifestyle that I work hard to cultivate. It means attending to details and dealing with small problems as soon as they surface. The benefits are enormous. One of the most noteworthy is that leaning in has cut down neurotic worrying so much that I actually miss it. Leaning in leads to the possibility that extreme tolerance is possible—because we aren't going to run away from the Eugenes of the world.

Inside that tolerance is a mix of self-acceptance and patience. It is a special form of patience, the kind that helps us, as my friend Mu Mun puts it, "shovel slow and steady." In Zen this means having time to respond to all of the life situations that get thrown our way. There is no need to rush. This antidote grew out of a long retreat in Chicago that I attended when I was a seminary student, working on the Zen koan "What is it?" For months I had been wrestling with the question, and it was kicking my butt big time. Every response I took into the interview room was flung back at me with a ring of my teacher's bell, throwing me out. Finally in one interview Sunim looked at me and said something like, "You have twenty-four hours. Go into the meditation hall and don't eat or sleep. Just do your practice."

So I did. At first I shouted the question. Then I cried with frustration. Then I whispered it, matching the rhythm of my steps. Then I lay on the floor and said it to the ceiling. For hours, only practice. Only questioning. At the end of the time period, nothing. I still didn't have a response.

When it was my turn for an interview the next day, I walked into the interview room and offered my resignation as a dharma student. I had failed. Sunim just looked at me. Then, with the softest voice possible, he said, "You have ten thousand years."

Ten thousand years? Suddenly all the pressure fell away. With ten thousand years I could just do my best in a relaxed, there-is-sufficient-time fashion. So I did. And the response appeared. Since then, whenever I tense up, trying to be more skillful, more tolerant, more trusting, I tell myself to relax because there is sufficient time to respond to the situation. Because it is true.

The third antidote is to remember or read words of encouragement from someone who has walked the spiritual path in earlier times. My man is Chinul, a wonderful Korean monk who lived in the twelfth century and had enough hardships in his life to make anyone want to run away to sex, drugs, and hip-hop. But he didn't. Instead he became a great wise man, weaving different Korean schools of Buddhism into one beautiful tapestry. Along the way he gave advice to the monks and nuns that, in a word, glowed. Here's a sample:

> *Strengthen your will; reprimand yourself; reprove your own laziness. Know your faults and turn toward what is good. Reform and repent your bad conduct; train and control your mind. Cultivate earnestly and the power of contemplation will grow; train continuously and your practice will become increasingly pure.... If you always remember your good fortune, you will never backslide. If you persevere in this way for a long time, naturally Samadhi and prajna will become full and bright and you will see your own mind-nature; you will use compassion and wisdom like sorcery and ferry across sentient beings; you will become a great field of merit.... I urge you to exert yourselves!* (From Robert Buswell's The Collected Works of Chinul, *p. 138*)

In this place tolerance comes naturally. In this place Eugene becomes the perfect teacher, a five-foot slurring mirror.

Restraint

Tolerance is related to restraint. When we don't exceed our limits, whether they are related to our bodies or our behavior, we are able to bring more tolerance into a situation than we otherwise could. Driving to Chicago one summer Sunday afternoon, I was stunned to hear a radio disc jockey yelling at his listeners. They would call in to explain a financial difficulty they were having, and his reaction was to lay in to them. What were they thinking! To get them out of their financial holes, he would give them blunt advice: "Cut up your credit cards and get a second job." "Sell your car and take public transportation." I was so surprised by his bluntness that I pulled the car over to the side of the highway to listen. Even when the listeners were sobbing, the man would not let up. They got themselves into trouble, and they could get themselves out. He would not compromise. When I got to Chicago and mentioned him to people, someone told me that 1.8 million people tune in to him each week. Why? Because we want to do better. We don't like these holes. We want out.

Given my own checkered financial past, I can tell you that the experience of climbing out of the hole feels wonderful. We feel better about ourselves and about our own capacity to keep a roof over our head and food on our table. Even better, we feel more optimistic about the world and the people living on it. A solid financial setback is humbling. If it can happen to us—and for most of us at some point it will—it can happen to anyone. Tolerance grows out of the understanding that we *all* face uphill climbs and we can all use some compassion and a hand when we find ourselves looking up from a gutter.

Writ large, respect, trusting ourselves, patience, and restraint create heroic figures. Think Martin Luther King Jr., Desmond

Tutu, Mother Teresa, or anyone you know who has those quali-
ties. For me the person who comes the closest to having all four
all the time is the poet and playwright Ron Allen. Growing up in
one of the toughest neighborhoods in Detroit, the former Black
Panther knocked drug addiction right out of his system. Today, in
his early fifties, he faces the complications of diabetes and kidneys
that apparently decide on a daily basis whether or not they want to
function.

   In the five years I have known Ron I have never seen him be
anything but tolerant. In the face of racist remarks that I cannot
believe continue to come out of people's mouths, he is tolerant. In
the face of grant rejections, apartment problems starting with no
heat, and a medical system that feels increasingly like a hallucina-
tion, Ron just keeps writing and producing plays and teaching
poetry and feeding the homeless men and women that the rest of us
have mostly forgotten. He has become more than a role model; he
is my true north for tolerance. More than once I've caught myself
asking, "What would Ron do in this situation?" Most recently I
asked myself the question when a neighborhood man decided that
I was his worst enemy and started yelling at me every time he saw
me. Usually I was a "fucking honky" followed by "fucking cunt."
Living in an inner city, I was usually pretty good at ignoring such
endearments. One day, though, he had really had it with me. He
was drunk, and I was afraid that he would fall backward off the
steps of the porch as he followed me to the door. When I reached for

the doorknob he suddenly stopped yelling, pulled down his pants, and mooned me.

In that moment I asked myself, "What would Ron do?"

Laugh. He'd laugh.

So I did. And asked the man if he wanted an apple or a banana. Even though he said, "Fuck you!" as he pulled his pants back up, he never yelled at me again.

four

THE FOURTH INGREDIENT:

A Capacity to Keep Going
—with Gusto

You can do anything you want to do. I mean it. Blunder ahead.

—Robert Henri

On any spiritual path, it takes guts to keep going. Instead of forging ahead, we want to cling to the life we know, even when it may be harming us. At least it is comfortable in its familiarity. Not that I mean to nag here, but if your life isn't a chocolate cake equivalent, you deserve better.

Back to Detroit. The rats in Still Point's Detroit neighborhood are bigger than three-month-old kittens. And they eat anything—food, wood, tires, plastic. They killed two of our chickens and almost got a third one before we screened in the entire chicken coop. Almost a million people live in this city, once rich, now increasingly abandoned. A reporter on National Public Radio said that one person between the ages of eighteen and twenty-four moves out of Michigan every forty minutes. My guess is that most of them are leaving from the ten-mile radius around Detroit. Postindustrial America has few jobs for inner-city folk, geniuses included. We're trading people for rats.

In a neighborhood that is 80 percent African American and surrounded by and infiltrated with crack houses, abandoned public housing, and structures falling in on themselves, there is still community. People greet each other on the street, give each other food, share clothes and blankets. We mourn shared losses and laugh together at television shows that give us a break from the sheer intensity of urban life. *Monk. American Idol. The Parkers.*

We meditate together, sometimes as many as seventy of us at a time. We teach each other about death and dying and parenting and how to really see a leaf so we can draw it. We are Christian, Jewish, Muslim, Buddhist, and label free. We write poetry together.

None of these things, however, helped the rat problem. When I first spotted two or three a day trying to sneak into the chicken house, I asked the neighbors for advice:

Neighbor one: "Shoot the fuckers."

Neighbor two: "Get some poison."

Neighbor three: "Call the city. No, forget that. They'll never show."

Neighbor four: "Shoot 'em."

The three of us then living at Still Point agreed that shooting was out of the question. This included BB guns. As for the poison, it causes a slow, painful death. Also vetoed. The three of us had taken the vow to "do no harm," rats included. So we sat with the problem for a while, watching the rats. And realized the simple truth that where there was no garbage—aside from the chickens—there were no rats. (Writing this, I'm embarrassed that it took a while to get this. The things I never learned in graduate school continue to haunt me.)

Have I mentioned that Still Point's neighborhood is covered with garbage? Three blocks away from a highway, subsidized housing, and a grade school, the streets are literally covered with garbage, especially in winter. Mostly the trash is made up of McDonald's wrappers, potato chip packaging, school papers, and cheap liquor bottles. It probably looks beautiful from the sky, all reds and golds and shiny.

So we hit the streets, picking up garbage several days a week. The task isn't in anyone's job description, but "rat problem" didn't appear in any of the house descriptions we looked at before moving here, either.

It takes a lot of energy to pick up garbage. But it feels good to do it. One November Sunday fifteen of us spent time clearing out the alley behind the house, two empty lots across the street, and the street that connects us with the grade school. We laughed and chatted and worked up sweats that would make a Bikram yoga teacher proud. We made it a contest. Everyone got to pick one piece of garbage to submit for the prize of a miniature tin garbage can filled with Reese's Pieces. The porch was filled with our bounty: old boots, blank high school hall passes, a whiskey bottle with a playing card stuffed into it. Because little kids were helping, we didn't put out the pornography we found, the business cards with names like "Hump."

The contest winner was a six-year-old girl, Maya, who found a hero action figure in the grasses of one of the lots. We cheered and clapped for her. She shared her winnings. And we all left filled with energy and a sense of possibilities for Detroit. That's what energetic effort does.

The Company We Keep

If we are to keep moving into a sweeter life, who we spend time with matters. My friend Joy Messick, a Sufi teacher extraordinaire, has more energy than anyone I've ever met, except for Mary Jane Hilker. Together they are a weather front. They are like two little kids, always on the move, grin filled. Almost always belly laughing. No matter what we are doing together, whether it is drinking tea or planning a trip abroad to drop in on Indian saints, they are a blast. Their energy feeds my energy until we become a frigging science project of snowballing energy.

Energy feeds energy. I saw this all the time at the abbey. When one person started cleaning, the rest of us started cleaning. One day I decided to clean after a construction job, which meant dust-covered mud splats and plaster puddles. I figured it would take me the whole day to clean one floor. Within an hour Ango joined me. We had a great time predicting *American Idol* outcomes while we scrubbed the entire floor twice. Chapak Patrick Smith came home and started vacuuming. Then Buddhimant showed up with flowers for the room. We all felt great. And the energy kept growing.

In the middle of the fifth month of a long hard winter, everyone in the abbey woke up one morning and started cleaning. Andrea cleaned out the refrigerator. Bassara vacuumed. Chapak cleaned walls. Without planning to, I found myself making a pot of black bean soup using the odds and ends of vegetables Andrea found in the refrigerator that were on the verge of rotting. In my hunt for more vegetables I found a frozen loaf of Italian bread behind some broccoli in the freezer. After it was covered with garlic pieces and butter, the oven turned it into a garlic bread that would make a five-star restaurant proud. Because three of the people who live here don't eat sugar, I tried my hand at sugar-free peanut butter cookies, at the last minute putting M&Ms in them so people could pick them out of the cookies if they wanted to while the rest of us got our sugar fix. It was great fun to work, cook, and eat together. Energy fed energy without any of us planning any of it. The abbey got a special cleaning. We had a wonderful meal.

Simplicity

Simplicity also feeds energy. Whenever I lose my bearings from too much urban life, I head for Amish country—about twice a year. I know it is time for a road trip when I wake up one morning tired with a cranky-on-top-of-happy veneer after sleeping at least six hours. It's not lack of sleep that has driven me into the land of crankiness. Fortunately, just after my groan of recognition, a small

voice always surfaces. "Hit the road," it says. "Hit the road before
you do any damage." So I do.

The Amish were the first Zen Buddhists in the country, only
without the Zen and without the Buddhism. Okay, maybe some
Zen. Their history is as juicy as history gets. The Amish arrived in
the United States in the early seventeen hundreds and settled near
Lancaster, Pennsylvania. They were taking advantage of William
Penn's policy of religious tolerance. About 80 percent of the Amish
live in Pennsylvania, Ohio, and Indiana. Their principles, called
Ordnung, call for a plain lifestyle with no personal adornments.
Gender roles are well defined, rituals are long-standing. Whenever I
am in Amish country I am struck by the detached politeness on the
part of everyone I meet. The people are kind but not hooked in to
the world the rest of us know and sometimes love.

The Bible is the core of Amish life. Redemption comes from
two things: brotherly love and self-denial. I've heard stories about
barn raisings that make *Extreme Makeover* look like child's play.
A barn lost in a fire can be completely replaced by volunteers in less
than a week. Building by hand. If someone gets sick, neighbors and
friends take over working their farm until they are on their feet. In
the community, no one goes hungry or without shelter or medical care if it is needed. This ethos of kindness and generosity is a
reminder of what is possible in a community.

Apparently because they believe in adult baptism and are
unwilling to serve in armies, the Amish have been persecuted from
the time they first appeared on the historical scene. They have their

roots in the 1520s among the Anabaptists of central Europe. After 1648 they lived in Alsace, in France. Because they irritated the heck out of rulers the way independent thinkers can, they got thrown out of France in 1712. That's when our own sweet William Penn came to their rescue. He promised that they could have land and the freedom to live according to their own rules if they wanted it. Three thousand Amish believed him.

As we move into the twenty-first century, most Amish families are without telephones, electricity, or water and gas lines. They farm. They work incredibly hard from dawn to dusk. They travel in three kinds of buggies—a market wagon, a family buggy, and a two-seater called a courting buggy. You know you've reached Amish country when you start seeing little girls in white caps and men with extra long beards but no mustaches, and buggies.

Quilts were my introduction to the Amish world. A dozen years ago I went to a national quilt exhibit, which stopped me in my tracks for several reasons. I couldn't believe it was possible to sew stitches that were that tiny. Ditto for some of the quilt pieces. I had no idea that so many different patterns of material existed. How do people come up with all those designs? The rainbows of color on the quilts glowed. The love, patience, and effort that went into each one were obvious. To this day, how anyone manages to get four corners of different sizes of cloth to come together over and over is beyond me.

For me, the most amazing quilts were the simple ones. They were made of dark, rich, solid colors—purple, blue, green, and black. They stole the show, each one more beautiful than the last.

As I stood staring at a group of them, a woman standing next to me told me they were made by Amish quilters. We ended up talking a little, and when she learned I lived in Michigan she grinned. "Well, you are about four hours away from where these were made. You should go visit." So I did. And I do.

Each time I visit I come home filled with good energy and faith in possibilities, simply from being in the middle of their energy. Always a treat.

How to Visit Amish Country

Wake up early. Take a shower, and put on your most comfortable road trip clothes. These are clothes where blueberry stains won't matter. More on this later. Imbibe your favorite nonalcoholic drink. Eat some protein, and pack some more for snacks. If you are in Detroit, Michigan, get onto I-94 west. With a full tank of gas, try not to drive too much over the speed limit. These days you get about ten miles an hour over the limit as grace, but nobody knows when this will end, and when it does Michigan tickets are expensive. Don't be the fastest vehicle. Rumor has it that they are less lenient In Indiana. In Ohio, be prepared to give up your firstborn if you are stopped by a state police officer for speeding. (Okay, maybe it isn't that bad.) A little over two hours out of Detroit, start watching for I-69. Take it south to Route 6, and slow the heck down. Start gaping. In the spring, a good time for a road trip, you'll notice that the ground, which looked like one big blob of beige when you were tooling along at, say, seventy miles per hour, is actually covered with every possible shade of yellow to dark brown with some purples and a splash of green thrown in to make things interesting. The base color? Latte with dark chocolate undertones. If this makes you think of coffee or chocolate, there are little family-owned restaurants all over the place. Or McDonald's has good coffee. There are no Starbucks.

The sky is wide, a bare gray lifting into a clear baby blue with a little purple and pink at the edges. The trees? Browns and golds, stark naked, waiting for their leaves with the patience of any saint you can name.

Feel free to wave at the trucks and the truckers in this part of the country. Most will wave back, and all but one will smile. Since you are both moving he won't harm you; he just won't smile.

Suddenly you'll hit Amish country. Stores will sport handwritten advertisements for products like Fish Eye Wines. The first buggy will appear on the side of the road. It will be square, black, and pulled by a horse. On its back you'll see a big orange triangle, rimmed in bright red, asking you politely to slow down. When you do, you'll see more and more Amish life.

First, the women. They will all be wearing the same style of dress—a simple color with a black apron or maybe a gray one. Black shoes and stockings or, yum, bare feet. A woman at Amish Acres in Nappanee, Indiana, told me that most Amish women have only four dresses—one to wear, one that is dirty and needs washing, one for dressy occasions such as a wedding, and one for spare. If you really look you'll notice that all the dresses have the same pattern.

All the women I've ever seen also wear bonnets. None of them wear jewelry. Come to think of it, I've never even seen a watch on anyone. The little girls look like miniature versions of the women. I wonder why they aren't swamped by photographers on a regular basis, they are so adorable. You'll see.

The boys too are adorable. Dutch-style haircuts are topped with black or straw hats. Suspenders hold up pants, covering shirts that are a deep purpley blue or white. If you keep looking you'll probably see a couple of kids on scooters and maybe one or two teenagers on bikes.

The Amish houses tend to be large and well kept. With the clothes drying on long clotheslines, they are a photographer's dream. Many of them have vegetable stands in front of them, offering every-thing from fruits and vegetables to cheese and baked goods.

If the stands make you hungry but you drive past them too quickly to stop, look for a home-style restaurant. There you can expect your lunch or dinner to include chicken, mashed potatoes and gravy, homemade bread and jam, coleslaw, applesauce, pie, cookies, fruit salad, and coffee. Alternatively, you could drive straight to Amish Acres, which is right on Route 6, and buy a min-iature blueberry pie for three dollars.

If you don't stop to eat the pie, you are making a mistake. It will be too delicious to rush. And too rich to eat it all at one sitting. But at the same time, you'll never make it home without trying to finish it while driving. Because it is impossible to watch where you are going and eat Amish blueberry pie at the same time without spilling it down your front—believe me, I have tried for years—expect to drive home stained.

The pie is exquisite with the farm's ninety-five-cent coffee. You'll arrive home energized and ready to face whatever it was that you needed to run away from yesterday. All for the price of a tank of gas and some food.

The energy of the Amish is palpable. It shows up in the neatness of the houses and in the sheer size of the washes hanging on the lines to dry. It shows up in the beauty of the barns and the carefully ironed clothes worn by the children. It is there in the smiles and the giggles and the laughter you'll hear if you are driving with your windows down and the radio off.

• • •

The effects of putting effort, energetic effort, into whatever we are doing are enormous. We feel better. We look better. We look younger, if that matters. And we can find ourselves doing things we never thought likely because our bodies and minds are staying sharp. Energetic effort has a way of keeping our emotions more stable and more positive.

I'm depending on this form of energy to keep me in good enough shape to hike well into old age. Until then I'm using Elise as my proof that I'll be able to think of mountains as hikes that need taking even into my eighties.

I met Elise in Banff in the Canadian Rockies in 2002. Deciding I needed to see exactly what kind of physical shape I was in, I found Country Walkers and signed up for a six-day hiking extravaganza in

the mountains. We hiked the jewel-colored Moraine Lake. We circled
Lake Louise, or at least ten miles of it. We hiked the Plain of Six Gla-
ciers, stopping at a mountain teahouse for lunch. Green tea, peanut
butter and jelly on whole-grain bread, and apple crunch. We hiked
Bow Lake, Whiskey Jack Falls, Yoho Lake, and Jackson Lake. Elise
was the "older woman" on the trip—maybe in her midseventies. Just
thinking about her energy makes me smile.

Within the first hour of the group coming together, two things
became clear: I was the one on a tight budget who had to jury-rig
every little thing; and Elise was the person with the best gear. And
she knew how to use it. If there was an option for a longer hike, she
always took it. Every day I would glimpse Elise up ahead, never slowing down. Sometimes she carried the rest of us up the mountains in
her slipstream. And she was kind in the zaniest way possible. Elise
would randomly stop and give one of us advice or feedback we didn't
ask for. She told one couple to find a counselor. Another woman
needed to get a new job. One day she stopped and called me over.
"Larkin, what the hell are you doing spending your life as a monk?
You think we can't use someone like you on the outside?" Before I
could even react, she was back on the trail in the front of the group,
leaving me thinking hard about my choices. Wow.

Finding Energy

What if we stall out? What if our energy flags? Telling you to get
going again is too simple. So I'll tell you this: We all stall out
sometimes. For me it is usually at the end of a long gray winter. Not

only is my energy at an all-time low, I'm just plain cranky. And so is just about everyone else. Last winter was long, cold, and frustrating. People lost jobs, marriages, kids, you name it. At one point I counted them up: more people were mad at me than had ever been in my whole life up to then.

Some people were mad at me because I was taking Elise's advice and leaving Still Point. Some were mad because I was taking too long to leave. One person was furious because I didn't say anything in public about a woman who had been in a coma for years and was certifiably brain-dead. Some family members wanted to pull her off the medical equipment that sustained her breathing. Others didn't. Then the federal government moved in, resulting in a super-sized public fiasco. It wasn't enough that my heart broke for her family and that I was praying for her every day.

And it wasn't just me. At a local Target I heard a woman scream, actually scream, at the young woman at the register because the cashier had made a mistake and had to start over again adding up a big pile of Easter goodies. The couple in the next booth at a local coffee shop two days later were really having at each other over a misunderstanding about what time they were supposed to meet for dinner the night before. All of us sitting in that section of the restaurant could hear every word. It wasn't pretty. A man in the post office went ballistic (something I had never seen before in real life) when the woman behind the counter gave him the wrong information about the cost of sending out his overweight package. Okay, the clerk was off by fifty bucks. It wasn't like she had sawed off his leg. He shouted at her at the top of his lungs and started pounding on the Plexiglas, shouting for the manager. When I left, a few minutes into his rage, I could hear the woman being sick in the back room.

Walking home, I thought about energy and effort and how hard a spiritual path can get. Then I remembered another larger-than-life character from the Flower Ornament Sutra, named Diamond Banner (DB). DB shows up in the middle of the sutra, just about when exhaustion sets in for the main character in the story, a young pilgrim who is determined to fall into complete enlightenment sooner rather than later. DB is a breath of fresh air. When the other enlightening beings spot him, they let out whoops of joy and pat him on the head like sports teammates the world around.

And DB lets loose. He's like the dad in *The Incredibles*. He can't help but save us from our own sorry stories. He is determined to feed us energy so we can keep going. "Children!" he shouts. "Great enlightening beings have made inconceivable great vows, filling the cosmos, which will save your sorry behinds!" (Okay, not his exact words, but close.)

He then proceeds to list their dedication vows, the ones they are never giving up:

1. Dedication to saving *all* sentient beings
2. Indestructible dedication
3. Dedication equal to all Buddhas
4. Dedication to reaching all places
5. Dedication to inexhaustible treasures of virtue

6. Dedication causing all roots of goodness to endure

7. Dedication equally adapting to all sentient beings

8. Dedication with complete sincerity

9. Dedication unattached, unbound, and liberated

He finishes up by shouting that their dedication will be equal to the cosmos and that they'll keep their vows "without retreating, without ceasing, without wearying, and without stopping anywhere" until we get ourselves back into our respective saddles.

Why?

Because, DB responds, "The sun doesn't choose [who it will shine on]."

We all get to bathe in their vows.

five

THE FIFTH INGREDIENT:

Clearheadedness

*He who has eyes to see, let him see, and he who has ears to hear,
let him hear.*

—Jesus Christ

On my drive to Seattle, I decided to visit Mount Rushmore. Rolling across the plains, ready for the mountains, I was one day ahead of schedule thanks to Harry Potter tapes. Taking a break only between the long chapters meant that I was driving at least a hundred miles more than I meant to on a daily basis.

Mount Rushmore pops up out of nowhere. It isn't near a city but rather high up in the hills at the far end of South Dakota. I was driving west up a steep grade trying to keep to forty miles per hour, choosing to believe that Subarus don't slide backward easily, when suddenly George Washington, Thomas Jefferson, Abraham Lincoln, and Theodore Roosevelt were staring down at me out of the sky.

Their faces are huge, really huge. The park information brochure says that each one is approximately sixty feet from the chin to the top of the head. Their noses? At least twenty feet across. All granite. I wondered if I was the only person whose reaction to seeing them was, "How weird?"

And, okay, beautiful.

Apparently back in the 1920s the state historian (Do all states have historians? Was I on the road too long?) invited a well-regarded sculptor, Gutzon Borglum, to scope out the Black Hills to see if he could create a work of art that would honor the birth, growth, preservation, and development of this country. Gutzon agreed to take on the task with these words: "Let us place there, carved high, as close to heaven as we can, the words of our leaders, their faces, to show posterity what manner of men they were. Then breathe a prayer that these records will endure until the wind and rain alone shall wear them away."

How amazing that Borglum was able to create such massive faces out of stone—how he clearly saw them on the sides of the hills; how he knew exactly what needed to be done.

The faces took fourteen years and four hundred workers to complete. For most of the time every day the men had to climb 760 steps to "get to work," carting along the tools they needed. Just thinking about this makes meditation retreats sound like preschool effort. They used dynamite for 90 percent of the carving. It's a miracle that nobody died.

Mount Rushmore is worth the drive. The park alone is

beautiful enough to make the effort. The avenue of state flags was surprisingly moving, and once I found my way out of the parking lot into daylight, my first reaction to the park's buildings was that their design alone should win them some award. Granite and glass tucked into a little valley. The place made me want to see the movie *North by Northwest* again. One of the park rangers was quite stern about sticking to the trails when he caught me trying to see if I could get close enough to look up the presidents' noses. Maybe a Red Bull to start the day hadn't been such a great idea.

Standing there, I wanted to write poetry about the sheer grandeur of the place. Strong, clear poems to match the strong, clear air and overwhelming feeling of gratitude that something like Mount Rushmore even exists. I wanted to write haiku.

Haiku

Clearheadedness happens. As we start to live our lives from a place that embraces ethics and tolerance, the world becomes increasingly clear. Tolerance helps to keep it clear because we don't get so clogged up by opinions, impatience, righteousness. The capacity to keep going guarantees that the clarity will continue and grow.

Clearheadedness feels like the lifting of a headache that we didn't even know we had.

Surprising things can strengthen this clearheadedness. For me one of those things has been poetry, especially haiku. My first introduction to haiku showed up in the form of poems sent to me inside beautiful note cards. They were from a venture capitalist in

Chicago I had a teenage crush on in my midthirties. Smack in the middle of a high-heeled, high-powered, management consulting day, this card would appear in the afternoon mail. Each one would carry a simple poem. Although they weren't, unfortunately, love poems (the crush was one-way), they always stopped me in my tracks. Here is my favorite:

Need friends ever speak?
There's tea to taste, and windsong
From the garden trees.

The haiku reminded me to take a break to just breathe, and when I reentered my busy day it was always somehow sweeter and softer.

Probably the most famous haiku poet is a fellow named Basho who lived in Japan from 1644 to 1694. I'm guessing you've already read his best-known poem. Here is one version:

Old pond ...
A frog leaps in
Water's sound.

(William J. Higginson, The Haiku Handbook, p. 9)

The poem is like a telegram shouting at us, "Now! Now! There is nothing but right now! Don't forget!" We can see the ancient pond surrounded by massive old trees and rocks that have been there since the beginning of earth. We can see the clear water reflecting the rocks, the trees, and the clouds in the sky. Everything is quiet. It is summer. Suddenly the frog leaps, and boom! Sound is there, catching us in God's grace, in emptiness, in joy.

Basho's story goes this way: One day a spiritual master asks him the meaning of Buddha. Basho's response is exquisitely simple: "After the rain, the green moss gets wet."

Apparently the master is sufficiently pleased to ask him a follow-up question: "And before the rain?"

Basho's reply is his haiku. A frog jumping into an old pond, breaking the silence with a small sharp sound. Nothing is left out of the image. It is a complete world, a world where every sense is welcome.

Historically, haiku poems have been seventeen syllables in length, arranged in three lines. The first is five syllables, the second seven, the third five. The shortness of the poems forces listeners to focus on what is most important.

William Higginson, a well-known haiku scholar, teaches that haiku is the answer to the eternal "what":

> *This is the main lesson of haiku. When we compose a haiku we are saying, "It is hard to tell you how I am feeling. Perhaps if I share with you the event that made me aware of those feelings you will have similar feelings of your own." Is this not one of the best ways to share feelings? When we want to "reach" another person with our feelings do we just want to say, "I feel sad"? Or, "I'm happy." Unless we tell them what it is that makes us feel sad or happy, how can they share our feelings? In fact we automatically ask this very question, when friends say they feel happiness or sadness, pain or joy. "What*

*is it?" "What's the matter?" or "What put that smile on your
face?" Haiku is the answer to this "What?" (William J.
Higginson,* The Haiku Handbook, *p. 5)*

These simple poems powerfully pull us into seeing how extraordinary the ordinary is. For two years I sat in on haiku classes taught
by Koho Vince Anila in Detroit. Koho even looks the part of a poet,
with his bald head, scholar glasses, heavy dark eyebrows, and muscu-
lar body encased in the most patched meditation pants I've ever seen.
What gives his sweetness away is the twinkle in his eyes. He loves the
world and all its creatures even when he is scolding, even when he
weeps for the rest of us with our thoughtless mistakes and opinions.

When Koho teaches poetry he helps you tap in to all of the
senses—the smell of the incense in the air, the taste of tea, the
coolness of the room, the way the light from a window bounces off
a statue. He plays old tapes of poets on a boom box, then he reads
them, then he has us read them. Then he makes us write our own.

Koho starts an early exercise by giving us pictures to give us
ideas—photographs from old *Life* magazines, maybe, or old post-
cards. Then he goes for the jugular, passing around a bowl filled
with slips of paper. On each is an instruction: "Go outside and
write about what you can see from the front porch." "Write about
the shoes lined up outside the door." "Write about the first stone
you notice." "Describe the tiny geranium that has somehow managed to survive the first frost of the year." For me, the piece of paper
is blank. Where can I possibly start?

I am not a poet, but I give it my best shot. When the class regroups we discover that breathtaking poems have burst out of people so ordinary you wouldn't notice a single one of us if we passed you on a sidewalk. I am a little embarrassed because the simple three lines tell us so much about each other. The man who writes about the stone ends his poem looking for a breakfast beer. A woman has written about the tiny drops of dew on the geranium. They are its tears at the dying of the earth.

When it is my turn I stand up to read my poem:

> *White white white white white*
> *White white white white white white white*
> *With crispy edges*

The whole group laughs. They are happy that I have discovered painting since I clearly have no future as a poet. But we've been intimate together. We've shared now. We want more.

When Koho's classes end, people don't want to leave. They linger, talking poetry and poets. They share information, resources, e-mail addresses. They tell each other to watch for more poems in their live journals.

When I leave, I walk into a world that is usually there for me only after long meditation retreats. Everything is more acute: Sounds are more clear; colors are brighter and more complex. In familiar rocks I see patterns that I've never noticed before. The green flickers in the gray tiles on the meditation room floor. I want

to paint them in a painting. And in this now I am almost overwhelmed with happiness.

Sometimes I think the job of poetry is to remind us that this
wide-open way of experiencing life is always available if we just stop
and look ... really look. Stop and listen ... really listen.

We Have Everything

When we take time to do these things, we realize that we have
everything we need, even if we are spending our lives in a prison
cell. My friend Fred Reinhart taught me this. Fred, recently given
the Buddhist name Kwan Um, began writing to me four years
ago. Since then, through regular correspondence, we have become
good friends. He gave me sound advice for dealing with someone who was very angry with me, and I suspect that my news of
the world outside his prison walls entertains him a little. I don't
know why he is in prison. I only know that he has more than a
hundred years left in his sentence. Hopefully they won't be spent
in solitary confinement. Kwan Um has a way of finding himself
there because he keeps trying to break up fights. But if the years
are spent in solitary confinement, he'll be okay because he lives
mostly with his senses wide open in the "nowness" that I get from
poetry and meditation. The letters he sends me, from his own
teeny room with one teeny window and one teeny hour of outside
exercise a day, are long, lovely poems. Descriptions of his days.
When he is with the other prisoners, reports of the yoga classes
he teaches. Descriptions of how hard he and his fellow inmates in

the print shop are working, about the contest they won. Each time I am touched. Always he offers me support as well. "Keep going, girlfriend." "You are doing good work." "Don't give up." Each time I think, "How could I?"

I've discovered a secret about this nowness. In this place we can clean up our karma, the muck we've created in our lives that needs scrubbing. When we see clearly we don't need to whine about anyone else, to blame them, or to run away. We just need to see. And then start scrubbing.

• • •

A life in which all of our available senses are in play is magical. On Saturday mornings Detroit throws its arms open to the world in the form of a huge farmers' market called the Eastern Market. Blocks and blocks of city property are crammed full of plants, flowers, fruits, and vegetables just waiting to be taken home to a good family. The people-watching is stellar: all shapes and colors, not to mention sizes and ages, cram ourselves into the walkways between the stalls, pretending that we aren't checking each other out as much as we are eyeing the garden products.

Even in the dead of winter the Eastern Market cheers me up. The flowers of every conceivable color are breathtaking atop snow and concrete. And the prices! I don't know of anywhere else in this country where you can buy two dozen roses for ten dollars. They go fast. Three-foot piles of oranges, bananas, grapes, and apples and the hot apple cider sold in the center of the chaos makes me forget the stinging cold. Every view in sight could be a photograph or a painting or both.

People always smile and greet each other at the market. Strangers chat. It is a community brought together by our senses. Although I'd probably go to the market for the produce anyway, I mostly go to see an ancient man who, every week, stands on a curb selling the most wilted roses, geraniums, and Gerber daisies I have ever seen. But his grin is so wide and his eyes are so filled with a love of life that he is always surrounded by customers. Whenever I see him he stops what he is doing and just stares at me for what feels like five minutes. Then he always sighs. It is like Kabuki theater; both of us know what comes next. After the sigh it is always, "Oh, baby, if only I were younger. If only I were younger."

I always laugh. The retort is always the same: "Yeah, if you weren't ninety and I wasn't fifty we would dance the night away, right?"

"Oh, we would," he says. "We would."

We both laugh, and he goes back to his crowd of customers while I merge back into the crowd, headed toward the piles of fruit in the next building.

A week later I make excuses to go back, even though we don't need anything. And again my man and I grin at each other, imagining a night of dancing together. For a moment I can feel the wind and I can see the moon and, in his eyes, what a handsome young ladies' man he was. Remnants are still there. Last week I asked him if it would be all right to squint while I looked at him so I could see how handsome he used to be.

"Why, yes, do that."

As I squinted he started to squint back.

"You were really a handsome young stallion, weren't you?"

"Yes, and you are still beautiful, baby."

I am in love. These clearheaded, bighearted moments make life grand.

Clearheadedness is fed by spiritual practice, whether it is meditation, prayer, bowing toward Mecca, chanting, or whatever your practice is. If we stick to whatever tradition we are most comfortable in and do our best to keep ethical principles, sooner or later living smack in the middle of present tense happens. And with it comes a joy in the data pulled in by all of our senses, even when the data isn't good news. You start to experience almost everything as simply data. And you discover that you can actually stay upright in any situation you find yourself in. If you are quiet, out of this clearheadedness will come a knowing about what you can do to help a situation. Maybe it will be to hug someone who is hurting. Maybe it is squinting at an old man to help him to remember an almost-forgotten youth. Maybe it is participating fully in an argument without giving in to the urge to curse.

Everyone Is the Zen Master

In this place of clearheadedness, everyone is teaching you something. When I first realized this, I cringed. My mind immediately flew back to the early 1990s when I was living at the Ann Arbor Zen Buddhist Temple. I had been there only a few weeks. I knew who Samu Sunim

was, but I don't think we had formally met. One quiet summer afternoon I was alone in the temple, reading in my room. Suddenly I heard
a roar: "What is this!" Running downstairs as fast as I could to see
who had broken in to the temple, I skidded to a stop inches away from
Sunim. He looked as furious as a person can look and still breathe.

He barely glanced at me. Instead he kept shouting, "What
is this! What is this!" as he noticed things that were being done
incorrectly. It felt like he was mad at everything he saw. After
about ten minutes, just when I thought he was slowing down, the
final roar: "No kitchen matches on the altar!" And off he stomped
upstairs.

For years I didn't think that incident taught me anything
except how to get angry at a Korean monk who was clearly insane.
Looking back out of clear eyes, I see that he taught me a book's
worth of lessons of protocol in those minutes. The importance of
locked doors. Why we need to keep the temple clean at all times.
Where at least a dozen articles should be kept. What the top of an
altar should have on it, and where. And, best of all, how not to correct others. I couldn't hear a word he was saying at first because all I
registered in my brain was high-decibel shouting. It was only after I
calmed down and stopped fantasizing about clunking him over the
head with one of the Buddha statues (this took years) did I realize
how much he had taught me. He is a great teacher.

Or there is a monk named Anatta. In all the years I have
known Anatta I have never seen him angry. Not once. When people
are rude or unkind or shout obscenities, he never offers an angry

response. Even Brahana Sarah Addae, our own patron saint of patience, occasionally says something through gritted teeth.

I once asked him about it. Here are his words verbatim: "I'm happy and grateful no matter what."

The words would be meaningless if I didn't see how he makes them real every day. He is a teacher.

Babies are teachers. They are clear about being tired, hungry, wet, or dirty. We don't need to argue with them about it. What is, is. Pets are teachers. Our temple cats were constant reminders to slow down and, whenever possible, sleep on the floor or sit on a cushion where the sun is coming in through a window.

The Obvious Response

A surprising benefit of clearheadedness is the ability to make instant decisions. When we are responding to information unclouded by our own biases, we see instantly what is needed in a situation. Life becomes improv. I can't count the number of times I've walked into a situation thinking my role was one thing, only to aim myself in a completely different direction depending on the need of the moment.

In the spring of 2005 we held an art show for nine Detroit artists who took over a healing center for three days to sell their work. On opening night I left the abbey in my gray robes, expecting to spend the evening greeting visitors. Instead, for half of the evening I held a beautiful baby in my arms so her young (tired) mother could have a break—and so I could stare at the baby without apology. When her mother asked for her back, I spent the rest of the night washing dishes and teacups in the center's tiny kitchen because that was what was most needed. Up to my elbows in marginally hot water, I looked up at one point to see who had just stepped in to clean, seeing the need, and it was my dharma sister, Brahana Sarah Addae Pizzimenti. I laughed out loud. She is one of the most clear-headed people I know. Of course she would be in the kitchen.

The next afternoon, overhearing a group of young people say how much they had enjoyed the show, I was thrilled. And glad that I had been one of the kitchen crew who made sure each had a clean cup for the delicious tea.

THE SIXTH INGREDIENT:
A Penchant for Surprise

You must do the thing you think you cannot do.

—Eleanor Roosevelt

As generosity, ethics, tolerance, and clearheadedness mix together, our lives palpably shift. For example, we may find ourselves worrying less because we've somehow stopped being the center of our own little universe. Better, thank-yous usually start appearing in the form of generous acts toward us, and others tolerate our idiosyncrasies with less judgment.

Surprises become fun. We start to see them as markers for direction in our lives rather than as punishments or rewards. In fact, surprises become opportunities to practice living life more spontaneously and more intuitively. We get to draw on our innate wisdom, sometimes called crazy wisdom because it is rarely linear. Our lives lighten up since crazy wisdom can bring with it great laughter and play. As we play more, we give other people permission to play as well. In this place impossible things become possible. A war ends when walls are torn down and immediately replaced by playgrounds for all children. Ideas for inexpensive hovercraft grow out of a family reunion where engineers and artists match wits. A celebration dinner and two bottles of wine later, hovercraft designs are created that are so simple and elegant that the group can actually foresee the end of highway building since we won't need roads anymore.

Crazy wisdom offers us an opportunity to be thrilled to be alive, sharing a world that is endlessly fascinating. This is a world that is holy.

My father was the first person who taught me about crazy wisdom. From him I learned to recognize a deep wisdom that isn't obvious at first but if you keep watching brings a "wow" or a "brilliant."

In 1969 I was coming back to the United States after five years of living the good life in Sydney, Australia. I had lucked out when my parents chose the high school where I spent most of those years. Loreto, Normanhurst, was a combination boarding and finishing school for young women that assumed that its graduates would become leaders and not simply housewives, a revolutionary concept back then in Australia. In spite of skipping classes so I could spend days at the beach and a penchant for talking back to virtually every authority figure in New South Wales, I was elected school captain in my last year. It was a first for an American girl attending Loreto, and many of the other girls' parents weren't happy. But the nuns stuck by their, and the students', votes, spending a significant amount of time convincing several sets of parents that I wouldn't destroy the reputation of the school over the course of the next year.

It was my introduction to the world of politics. After Loreto I went to Sydney University for a semester before heading back to the States. There I learned about the war in Vietnam from a young political science professor who talked about the power of nations and the problems that surface when one country has so much power that it can impose its values and culture on other countries without being held accountable. He used Germany as an example. Then he talked about Vietnam and asked us to discuss the role of the United States in the war. Until that moment I had assumed that the war was black-and-white, with the United States clearly the white knight. But I became less and less sure as we read documents together. A friend introduced me to the songs of a young folk singer, Bob Dylan. On Friday nights, groups of us would crowd into someone's living room to hear Dylan and talk about the war.

A protest against militarism on campus was organized. It didn't matter that there were only twelve people in Sydney's ROTC program. We had a world to change. I remember the protest as a party with only one negative element. When my father heard about the protest on a radio news broadcast, he called to leave me the following message: If he saw my face on the television news coverage of the protest, I would lose my allowance.

The gauntlet had been thrown. At eighteen I was willing to take the risk of losing an allowance for a better world. Even so, I

was relieved that my smiling face apparently didn't show up on any
news broadcasts since the allowance kept coming all semester.

At the end of the semester I decided that I was too homesick
for the United States to stay away any longer. Arriving in New York
City, I landed smack in the middle of student protests against the
war. It didn't take much to decide that Columbia University was
where I belonged.

My father was furious. Whenever we saw each other we
would fight about Vietnam. I was meeting young women whose
brothers had been killed, and nobody could explain how the United
States had gotten into the fix in a way that helped me understand
the loss of lives. I gave Dad books and begged him to read them.
Johnny Got His Gun. The Ellsberg Papers. He would argue back, telling me that what the world really needed was a benevolent dictator
and that the United States was the only country that had the power
and heart to act in such a capacity.

We went around and around. Then I would go back to Bar-
nard, and he would go back to IBM.

One day he simply stopped arguing with me. We were about
a year into our fights, and I was trying to decide what I wanted
to do after college. Dad asked me to meet him for dinner at his
favorite bar in midtown Manhattan. I knew the purpose wasn't
to pull back on any financial support. He had already done that
when I decided that I wanted to major in political science instead of
mathematics. I had been warned that the money spigot would stop
if I made the change and had been willing to take the hit.

Walking into the restaurant, I contemplated why he wanted to see me. Maybe he was getting remarried. Or was dying. Or moving. Maybe he was doing all three. When I saw him and sat down at the table, he looked at me and ordered us a bottle of wine. So far not even a greeting. I figured I was in trouble. It was all I could do not to squirm right out of my chair. Maybe, I thought, he's found out that I tried marijuana and is going to have me arrested. As a brother of a Boston cop, he had that kind of loyalty to the legal system.

Instead he looked at me and said, "I was wrong."

I had no idea what he was talking about. Fortunately, I was too stunned to open my mouth, which gave him time to continue.

"I was wrong about the war. You kids are right."

Is it possible to be more stunned than stunned? If it is, that was me.

He had read the books, paid closer attention to the political policy speeches, the rising death count. He had asked people he knew in the government about the war. Since he was pretty high up in IBM's ranks, I guessed that the government people were pretty high up in political rank.

"There's no way we'll win."

I still couldn't talk.

He went on. "The system needs changing. I know you want to change it, but you are going about it the wrong way." What we needed was crazy wisdom.

Huh?

My father spent the rest of the night outlining a detailed strategy for how I could be a legitimate, verifiable change agent. It started with this: "Apply to get into a bank management training program."

"Instead of protesting?!"

It *was* crazy. My father had gone mad. Out of loyalty I stayed put, although I also put my glass of wine down for good. He methodically made his case. She who holds the purse strings holds the power. I could join a bank and work my way up through the ranks. Once I ran the bank—it never occurred to him that I wouldn't (dear old Dad)—I could become involved in policy making at a world level. I could use economic tools to break up dictatorships and to help build sustainable economies at the local level so people wouldn't be so susceptible to outside influences.

It was that simple, he said.

It was crazy. And wise. And while I didn't literally take his advice, I was able to see—through jobs as a program officer for a multinational philanthropic organization and later as a management consultant—how right on his advice was.

Crazy wisdom is intuition on overdrive. And fun. A guaranteed method for tapping in to it is to take up training with a Zen teacher, someone committed to driving you nuts by asking you seemingly meaningless questions until responses suddenly start floating up from your belly. Crazy responses. Crazy responses that are correct. In that moment you open the spigot to genuine wisdom and are filled with the grace of the ages.

Not to say that getting to that place is easy. Even getting to a
quiet place in meditation or prayer is hard work. Several years back
I led a retreat at the Leaven Center, a Christian retreat center in the
woods of central Michigan in the week before the official start of
spring. More than half of the eighteen women and two men who
committed themselves to two days of spiritual practice were new to
meditation. Ringing the meditation bell for the first formal sitting
on Friday evening, I cringed, knowing how surprised they would be
at how tough it is to sit still for thirty minutes. Tough on their bodies. Tough on their brains.

Sure enough, at the end of the first night when I asked the
group how they were doing, one woman said she felt nauseated. She
was also having trouble breathing. "It's fear," I told her. "Your mind
doesn't like being watched. It will get used to it. Honest." Several
people nodded. I went on. "It's hard to watch how nuts we are."
More nods.

We kept at it for seven hours on Saturday. At the lunch break,
the woman who had felt ill told me she felt much better. Still, the group
was clearly tired by the end of the retreat. They'd had a taste of quiet,
but would it be enough to motivate them to sit back down on a cushion
at home? Or to simply take time out of each day for formal prayers?
To thank Jesus, say? I wanted to bribe them, to promise big, colorful
miracles, the kind that would make the cut for a *People* magazine story
or at least *Good Housekeeping*. I wanted to tell them, "Look for the rainbow that will be in the sky as you drive home." But I couldn't get the
words out of my mouth even though it had been raining and odds were

that at least one rainbow was out there somewhere. Instead, I read from
D. T. Suzuki, one of the first Buddhist teachers to come to the United
States with Zen in his pocket. He did promise miracles:

> *Having set ourselves free from the misconception of Self,*
> *we ... awaken our innermost wisdom, pure and divine....*
> *It is the divine light, the inner heaven, the key to all moral*
> *treasures, the source of all influence and power, the seat of*
> *kindness, justice, sympathy, impartial love, humanity, and*
> *mercy, the measure of all things. When this innermost wis-*
> *dom is fully awakened, we are able to realize that ... life is not*
> *an ocean of birth, disease, old age and death, nor the vale of*
> *tears, but the holy temple of Buddha, the Pure Land, where he*
> *can enjoy the bliss of Nirvana.*
>
> *Then our minds go through an entire revolution. We are no*
> *more troubled by anger and hatred, no more bitten by envy*
> *and ambition, no more stung by sorrow and chagrin, no more*
> *overwhelmed by melancholy and despair.* (An Introduction
> to Zen Buddhism, *p. 10*)

I hoped they'd get it. I wanted them to be happy.

What Is It?

Samu Sunim used a koan—"What is it?"—to help his students
slice through the crazy-making gunk of our lives so we could be
clearheaded, compassionate, and wise. It took me five years to even
come close to understanding the question, let alone respond to it.
But when I finally did, a different way of living my life appeared—
moment by moment instead of staying caught in the net of long-

term plans. It is a terrific question. Sunim told me that once I really understood the power of the question, including the act of questioning, I would know exactly how to respond to any situation in my life. Even death.

He was right. During the days when "What is it?" is a song in my head, contentment is mine, even on the days when Eugene used to pound on the front door with all his might, asking for a banana and an empty pop can for the fifth time before noon. Telling him that we don't drink soda pop in the mornings and that I just gave him the three cans left over from the weekend doesn't mean he's done asking for the day. He'll be back. When my questioning is strong, I simply wave him away at the next pounding. When it isn't I yell at him, hard.

Brahana

I love koans. They pull crazy wisdom right out of us. I used them at Still Point during my tenure. About twenty people regularly showed up to work through them. One is Sarah Addae Pizzimenti. We know her as Brahana. A Detroiter, Brahana is by turns a loving partner, mother, poet, artist, chef, and friend. She is one of only three people in the sangha who understand carpentry. Brahana works tirelessly at her practice. She is a mother of two young children and a couple of older ones, and her days overflow. She supports her husband's chiropractic practice, sells homemade soup at Avalon Bakery, teaches when she can. I've never heard her yell in anger. Even when she is completely surrounded by chaos she is fully present, doing the next obvious thing, filled with good cheer.

When Brahana first started showing up for interviews, I was struck by her quiet. She *was* peace. Nothing I said or did fazed her. Nothing. Outside of interviews, during her life as a seminary student, she did her spiritual practice without complaint. While other students made excuses for not waking up at 6 a.m. or missing evening meditation practice, Brahana just did the work. On some days this meant waking up in the middle of the night to sit. On others it meant waiting until everyone in her busy household was fast asleep—invariably well past midnight. Over the years she has shown up for early morning practice at the abbey more than anyone else in the sangha. When the time came for her ordination, Brahana shaved her head without blinking, even though shaved heads for Still Point dharma teachers is not mandatory.

Brahana's eyes shine and her laughter is instant, and she knows how to let go of the things she can't affect. In the sangha I watched her skillfully decide, moment by moment, when an issue needed attention and when it was wiser to simply drop it. When an opportunity to go on a pilgrimage to Korea surfaced out of the blue, she immediately decided that she wanted to go and started raising money. At the same time, she blew through all the interview questions I could throw at her until we were playing together: dharma combat for girls. She is the person I turned to for advice when a board member decided that I'd screwed up or when a seminary student decided that I was the worst thing that had ever happened to him—worse than his mother, whom he had just realized he would be furious with if he hadn't been so fixated on me. Just being in the same room with Brahana calms me down.

In the winter of 2004 the sangha decided to help her to raise the transportation costs for her pilgrimage by throwing her a dharma combat party. We got to ask her anything about Buddhism.

It was a Friday night, and Brahana was sitting in front of the altar in the meditation hall in her formal robes, candles lit, incense burning. Her pale wooden begging bowl rested at her feet. There were already two dollars in it, and we hadn't even started yet. Brahana was determined. She was willing to bare everything—her heart, her Buddha nature, her humanity—for this trip. Her will to go permeated the room.

Airfare was expensive—maybe eight hundred dollars. None of us had the money to give her. Actually, none of us had much money at all. Most of us lived month to month. Plus, Brahana wanted to help three of her dharma sisters go with her. None of them had the money either. While Still Point's board had given me permission to pay for up to five hundred of each woman's expenses, that would only cover their costs once they hit Korea. The plane trip expense loomed large.

It was the end of another long, cold, winter week. We were all happy to be together, warm and full of vegetarian potluck offerings. Excitement filled the room. We love this young woman.

Sitting on cushions, forty of us crowded around her, ready to pounce. I reviewed the ground rules. We could ask her anything related to dharma, the wisdom of Buddha, and other enlightened teachers. She would spontaneously respond out of her awakened heart. We would see her crazy wisdom in action. We would put money or an offering into her bowl reflecting our level of satisfaction with her response.

It was a tough crowd. Rinzai students from other traditions had come—a visitor from California, another from South Dakota. A Native American shaman. A monk who is known for trapping people in their delusions, going for every jugular he sees with little kindness.

It took us a couple of minutes to settle. If she stretched, Brahana could touch ten of us. I sat beside her.

"Questions, questions," I announced. "Come forward with any question you have."

No one moved. So I went. Kneeling in front of my friend, I bowed, then asked,

"Does a dog have Buddha nature, yes or no?"

She responded, "Does a dog have Buddha nature, yes or no?"

I barked, and we were off and running.

The questions came in spurts. "What do children know?" A three-year-old asked, "Why are dinosaurs so big?" When she got her answer, she put her offering in the bowl. It was a doll.

Some questions were a plea for advice. From a young mother: "How can I find the time for practice?"

Brahana looked into the woman's heart. There was silence. Then, "When you clean . . ." and Brahana started chanting.

"*Sugamuni Bul, sugamuni Bul ...*" Her voice was angelic. We were transfixed. She continued, "When you cook ... *Buddha, Dharma, Sangha.*" She was still chanting. I was in tears. I could hear other people sniffling. We could feel Brahana pouring energy into the young woman right then and there. It was a moment moving beyond words.

"Questions, questions."

Ango jumped up. He wore plastic glasses with googly eyes. Kneeling in front of Brahana, he bowed, pushed her bowl out from in front of her, and set the glasses down.

"What is this?" he said loudly. "If you say it is a pair of googly eyes, wrong! If you say it is not a pair of googly eyes, wrong!"

Brahana looked at him and grinned. Before we knew it, she had put them on and was bouncing around on the cushion, a wild woman. Everyone laughed. For extra credit she shot Ango with a rubber band. By then we were laughing so hard some of us were coughing.

Koho knelt in front of her. He was sincere. His wife was going to have a baby in two months, their first. It was to be a little girl. What could he do so he didn't feel ownership of his daughter? So much attachment troubled him.

Brahana just looked at him. "Will you die? Will you get old?"

He bowed, understanding. Some things just happen, no matter how we try to avoid them. He will adore his daughter. He did already. His concern for her safety, combined with love, will create attachment. We all become attached to the people, places, animals, things we love. As Brahana spoke to Koho, an old story flashed through my head. It was about an ancient Zen master who apparently had no attachments, but when the temple cat died he sent a note to his student: "The cat died." When the student saw his handwriting, she knew how much he missed the little animal and promptly went out to find him a kitten to keep him company.

Our tendency is to love our children with a deep attachment. Buddha was so sensitive to this that he named his son Rahula, which means "hindrance." In my life, Sunim called my daughter, Jamie, my "last piece of baggage." She would hold me back, he said. My love for her would slow my spiritual unfolding. He was right. Parenting is a steep price. I would pay it a million times over. So would Koho—and Jaya hadn't even made it to the world outside of her mother's womb. He already loved her that much.

The shaman stepped forward. Hand held up to hers, he looked intently into Brahana's eyes. And stayed there. I watched her let him see inside of her. There is no bottom. He smiled, pleased. More money went into the begging bowl.

A handful of questions later, we were done. The formal finish was to bow to each other. We bowed to Brahana. She bowed to us. It wasn't enough. We cheered, clapped, and shouted. A full-hearted, full-throated, spunky mama Buddha had just blessed the hell out of Still Point.

In the bowl, $1,051 and five dolls.

Brahana was going to Korea.

seven

THE SEVENTH INGREDIENT:
Adventuring

Fill what's empty. Empty what's full. Scratch where it itches.

—Alice Roosevelt Longworth

*I*t is not a good idea to rely on one book on tape while driving across America. I never thought I would say this, but it will be okay to wait awhile to listen to the next Harry Potter book, even though I love Harry's new crankiness. I was dreaming Harry Potter dreams for days after I finished the last chapter. And by the time I reached the West Coast, every part of me hurt. A massage wasn't going to cure the aches. I needed to run a marathon or something. How do those truck drivers survive?

I never wanted to see the inside of a McDonald's again. Ever. Ditto for Starbucks. They did what they needed to do. They got me across the country.

At the same time, that drive reminded me that living life as an adventurer, with little ahead of us neatly laid out, is a total blast. I had forgotten that this much freedom is fun, not scary. As a bonus, I came up with at least a dozen ideas for books, two products, and a play. I met a dozen unforgettable people. Topping the list is the pharmacist in Montana, an adorable aging hippie with diamonds everywhere. Plus, he gave me mega-drugs for a wicked toothache for less than twenty bucks.

I realized that I love, love, love being middle-aged. I get to watch the world without having to worry about finishing college or what I'll be when I grow up. Instead, I get to see which doors open and which ones close so I can be useful as one of the country's elders.

• • •

To take risks, we need to trust that we will survive them— that new people, new places, and new behaviors won't kill us any more than not taking risks will. This type of trust forces us to open our eyes wide to that new date, new mountain in front of us, the brand-new mountain bike. When we do, an appreciation for them grows. The person isn't a stranger anymore. The mountain, scaled, will become a lifelong memory. The bike will be our modern-day horse, taking us into places we would never have experienced otherwise—deserted desert trails, isolated beaches, forgotten mountain passes. And the more risks we take, the more adventures we step into, the more we appreciate the experience of all of our senses.

Appreciation writ large becomes a form of impersonal love and respect, the kind you feel walking into a medieval cathedral or the Taj Mahal or looking into the eyes of a Native American shaman. The world becomes holier before our very eyes. And as it does, our life becomes sweeter, each moment precious.

• • •

My friend Joe Dahl had the best pickup lines of anyone I have ever met. During my late twenties, a group of my women friends convinced me that we could have fun running together in a pack through the streets of Portland, Oregon. We weren't very fast since the purpose of our runs was to gossip. At the end of a fine spring morning run, we spotted a poster for a half marathon that would weave through the city's downtown streets and on to the waterfront. Without thinking, we signed up. Although none of us had ever run more than three miles, we figured our group energy combined with the fear of being teased for the rest of our lives if we didn't finish meant that we could do the thirteen-plus miles.

What we didn't know is that it is a bad idea to drink three cups of tea before you start.

By the fourth mile of the race, all any of us could think about was finding a place to pee. Finally I spotted a bar that was open for business, apparently so onlookers could sit comfortably watching the mass of runners passing by.

Expecting my friends to join me, I signaled that I was heading over, only to be waved off.

"See you at the finish line, Larkin!"

Half running into the bar, in a noble effort not to lose much time, I asked if I could use the restroom. The bartender, who is hopefully spending his days in hell right about now, replied with one word: "No."

"No?!"

"You have to buy a drink."

"Okay, give me a ginger ale."

I sat on a bar stool, sweaty legs coming out of sweat-soaked shorts.

"You know what? Make it a Shirley Temple. And if it is okay, I'd like three cherries."

To the amazement of everyone near me, I went to the bathroom, came back, and slowly sipped the drink. By now I was sweating steadily, that sweating that hits when your body thinks you are done exercising. I knew the nine-minute mile was no longer mine, so there was really no need to stay worked up about the race.

When I was done with the drink—and this included eating every last ice cube—I got up to use the bathroom again. When I emerged refreshed, partially scrubbed clean, and ready to run, a cute dark-haired man, maybe thirty, stood in my path.

"When you finish the race, come back and I'll buy you lunch."

"In these?" I looked down at my Salvation Army shorts, top, and running shoes.

"In those."

"I'm running with three friends."

"Bring them."

Joe Dahl. He bought us a huge lunch. That bar is probably still spraying down the booths to get rid of our sweat. The two of us got along famously, especially once I learned that he was the Northwest distributor for an elite brand of ice cream, then my favorite food on the planet.

At the end of the lunch, when he asked me to go out with him on the following Friday night, mine was an easy yes. And when he never showed up, it only took me a couple of phone calls to track him down in Portland's ice cream plant. Instead of asking for him, I asked the dispatcher if he could simply leave a message over the loudspeaker system for me. A good friend of Joe's, he was happy to comply.

The message: "You can leave me, Joe, if you must. But no matter what you say or do, I am keeping the baby."

The next morning there was ice cream outside my apartment. Could we try again?

And while we both quickly realized that we were not mate material, Joe taught me how to live life as a wild adventurer, because that is what he is. And along the way he taught me about the possibilities of friendship. And how being a true friend is its own adventure because we can never really know where a friendship will lead.

The man is fearless. When he fell in love with a young woman who didn't notice him, he bought her a pair of Tony Lama cowboy boots and left them on her doorstep, just because. Even though he knew, he really knew, that she was always going to be his personal version of Charlie Brown's red-haired girl, he fell in love anyway. And took on heartbreak like it was a wild bronco that just needed riding. I was in awe.

Joe taught me that trying new things simply for the sake of trying new things is its own reward. And that we can always pick ourselves up and dust ourselves off, even when we almost die from being caught in a collapsed car on fire. Joe barely survived that one. He taught me that a house doesn't have to be on land and that houseboat communities are simply extended families that are never, ever boring. He taught me that big houses are like extra pounds. Just dragging them around takes too much work.

Joe taught me to pay attention to what really matters. And that a good friend will point us in the direction of the best adventures ever. More than once he picked me up and brushed me off. He bailed out my son. He told me the truth. He loves me with the kind of permission that gives me the green light I need to dye my hair bright red and get my first tattoo. If life can't be a great adventure, how can we learn the lessons we need to learn? We'll be too scared to look. Even if the adventure is trying a new food or a new route to work or learning how to play bridge, it will feed the deepest part of us. It will open our hearts somehow.

Joe taught me that if we really love something, it is okay to learn everything we can about it, to roll around in a cloud of curiosity about it, to ask questions, to find experts. This means getting out from under books and DVDs. It means heading into the mouth of whatever we are fascinated by, to experience it with all our senses.

A few years ago Joe decided that he wanted to visit every major baseball stadium—especially the old ones before they were foolishly torn down—to see a game in each, and to eat its food. The man loves baseball the way I love my kids. He knows more about baseball than I know about everything in my life put together. Statistics. Players. Even the stadiums. Even the food in the stadiums. And of course the beer. He spent half a year on these visits, as I recall. He got to know many of the big name players personally, becoming quite the groupie, and ate at least one hot dog at each ballpark.

Joe doesn't look back. He just does his best. He isn't perfect and knows it. He doesn't even try. He gives his friends permission as well to give up the quest for perfection. He doesn't regret. He doesn't hold grudges. He is a one-man learning machine and the person who lights up a room with his grin and out-of-body charisma.

• • •

Wild adventurers are everywhere. We just need to notice them and watch how they appreciate the world and everything in it. We can see how their own crazy wisdom has led them down wonderful unplanned paths. Another example is Judy Wicks. I found out about Judy Wicks through Urban Outfitters. When the store moved to Ann Arbor, I was so taken by its eclectic feel and smart-aleck style that I asked the manager about its history. He told me that it grew out of a store called Free People's store. Judy Wicks was one of its founders. A week later (*Twilight Zone!*) I saw an article about her, how she lost everything in the 1970s and ended up being a waitress, and later a manager, during thirteen years at La Terrasse in Philadelphia.

Here is where her adventurer spirit kicked in big-time. At the end of her tenure at La Terrasse, Judy ran a little muffin shop on the first floor of her house. One day she realized that more and more people were finding her—and that the muffin shop was a business that could support her. That shop is now called the White Dog Café, world famous in foodie circles.

While it is true that the café is an active community center, hosting celebrations, author signings, and political events, a quiet revolution is also going on. The café is powered by wind. Meats and vegetables come from local organic farmers. When the farmers didn't have money to grow what she needed, Wicks loaned them seed capital. I'm told that 20 percent of the restaurant's profits go toward supporting other nonprofit groups. She holds pajama party brunches. Judy is surrounded by friends and fellow adventurers, and as far as I can tell, she doesn't look back.

• • •

Giving yourself permission to be an adventurer—whatever that means to you—feeds you in the deepest way possible. You will be energized. Wisdom grows out of your experiences. So does compassion. If you don't believe me, go read stories of wild adventurers for yourself. I say start with the ancient heroes. What the heck, start with the first one, Gilgamesh.

Gilgamesh fought his way out of arrogance and into wisdom some 2740 years ago. Nobody even knew his story until about 150 ago, when a young British explorer found a bunch of clay slabs with the hero's story on them. Rumor has it that the British curator who first translated the stories was so excited by them that he stripped and danced around his museum completely nude in an explosion of emotion.

It is a great story.

Gilgamesh is an arrogant young king who has everything he could possibly want. Women. Men. A huge plasma television. Stock in Google. But he is lonely. Happily, through a series of fights he meets a sweet character named Enkidu, who becomes his best friend. They are soon inseparable, getting into all kinds of mischief, much of it hilarious. Through Enkidu, Gilgamesh learns about compassion and grief and wisdom and how to keep holding up the world even during his worst days.

Genuine friendships feed this adventuring. I watch Ango Neil Heidrich and Koho Vince Anila. They are great friends. They love each other. Ango holds Koho up. Koho holds Ango up. They tell each other their deepest secrets, their deepest fears. They cry together, and they laugh until they can't breathe. They go on pilgrimages together. When I asked Koho to write about Ango for the Still Point newsletter, he gave me this:

REFLECTIONS ON A TRUE MONK

It's our first time in Korea, and I'm tagging along with Ango up and down "Buddhist Articles Street" in Seoul, looking for a place to get robes made for sangha members back at home.... Our first morning, having warmed ourselves in the tent of a street food vendor, we start at one end of the street looking for a place to get the robes made. The shops quickly become indistinguishable from one another—let's face it, available in many colors and styles Dharma robes ain't, and with slight variations the prices seem pretty standard too. Still jet-lagged and a bit disoriented, we've been up since 3 a.m.

and could have easily researched a small handful of shops, ordered nice robes, and had the day to unwind. But it's soon apparent that Ango intends to visit every store, inspecting the robes, their materials and craftsmanship, talking with shop owners, and jotting things in his little notebook. At the end of the street we find what Ango has been looking for: simple robes, impeccably made of the highest-quality materials. Perfect for the folks at Still Point. Ango spent the next three hours explaining the measurements for fifteen sets of robes and cashing traveler's checks at the bank down the street. I'm being neither poetic nor sentimental in saying that I'd just spent the whole day learning some of what it means to love and nurture a sangha.... I doubt a day will go by without the deepest gratitude for what Ango has done for this sangha and for our practice. And also, perhaps, not a day will pass when I don't ask myself at least once, "What would Ango do?"

Ango, it's no secret that I love you. Dearly. What you may not know, though, is that in this practice, which is ideally without goal, I secretly hope to someday be like you. Every evening when you're chanting in some big Buddha Hall in Korea, we'll be doing bows for you in the morning at Still Point. Yer m'boy, Blue!

The friendship of these two young men is not based on sports or women or other men. It is based on compassion and loving-kindness. It keeps them on a spiritual path and feeds the adventurer in both. It gives them the courage to embrace crazy wisdom. And it helps them to be available to the rest of the world, that is, you and me.

When I watch people turn their lives into the lives of adventurers who then open their hearts to the world, it is thrilling beyond words. It is as though they step up to take care of the rest of us in numberless ways. Ann offers to pick Liz up every Sunday for church. Ron Allen reads a scripture with such passion that it feels like God's own voice is filling the room. Everyone becomes our friend. It can feel a little weird at first. The crossing guard who never seemed to notice us starts shouting a "Good morning!" across four lanes of traffic. Even when they don't start out as a friend, each person we come into contact with somehow morphs into one.

Many of the miracles of our lives happen in this place of friendship. My daughter, Jamie, says it is okay to give Koho her car. She won't be needing it in Wisconsin, and he needs a way to get to and from Detroit on the weekends. For months an abbey resident saves a little money out of each week's paycheck for a friend about to embark on a pilgrimage. Another friend finds himself in a long line at the grocery store. Everyone in front of him is cranky, tired from a long week. About half of them aim their irritation at the grocery clerk. When he gets to the front of the line, he apologizes for all of them and tells her he noticed how patient she was with each person. The smile of her reaction lights up her whole face. Koho is having breakfast at a café when a man sitting a couple of tables away gets up to get change for a newspaper. Before he gets it, Koho gives him one. In return, when Koho gets up to pay for his breakfast he discovers that the man, who has left the restaurant ahead of him, has paid for his meal.

Adventurers and Friendship

Ours is a world of friendships. We love them; we want them. And they aren't limited to humans, as any pet owner knows. In the Jataka collection of tales about his lives before he made it to the human realm is a story about Buddha when he was a parrot. This parrot, a beautiful green, red, and yellow creature, lived in a fig tree that he loved very much. Basically, he was a happy little bird in a happy little tree. "I'll never abandon it for another refuge" just about sums up the relationship.

For a long time the little parrot and the fig tree have a wonderful time living together. But one day, the king of the gods, Shakra, gets bored, the way kings of gods have a tendency to do. He decides that he wants to see just how strong this parrot–fig tree friendship is. That day he makes the tree dry up. Its leaves fall off in a huge clump, until all that is left is a collection of scrawny, naked branches. They aren't going to do the parrot any good on hot days. Every day is a hot day.

The parrot doesn't care. He sits on the branches when the sun isn't too strong. And when it is, he flies in circles around his friend the tree, making a breeze for both of them. "Should friends part just because bitter fortune has struck? Days pass and for-tunes change. And my tree, I'll not leave you" (*The Hungry Tigress*:

Buddhist Myths, Legends, and Jataka Tales, as told by Rafe Martin, pp. 63–64).

And he doesn't. He keeps the naked fig tree company every single day until Shakra finally decides that the parrot isn't kidding about the friendship. The tree gets its leaves back and then its fruit. Rumor has it that Shakra throws in a pure blue sky as an extra bonus. Friendships can do that to a god.

• • •

Even the most heartbreaking events demonstrate the power of this loving-kindness. In the summer of 1994 a seven-year-old boy named Nicholas Green was visiting Italy from California with his family. He really loved Italy, the theatrical aura of the country, its exuberance, the love Italians have for children. If you saw a picture of Nicholas, you would think "boys' choir." Rosy cheeks, thick golden brown hair, a button nose, freckles.

One night, driving through the toe of the country sometime after midnight, his father noticed a car coming up fast behind them. Suddenly the car pulled up beside their vehicle, and a man started shooting, Although Nicholas's father managed to drive away from the other car, when he was finally able to stop to see how everyone was doing, he discovered that Nicholas had been shot.

All of Italy tried to save him. A stranger drove the family to the hospital, handing Nicholas's father his rosary. Whole police forces cleared the way for the family. Strangers came to sit with

them while they waited to see if the boy would survive. Hordes of
teddy bears showed up.

When Nicholas died, the country wept.

As a parent, I could understand his family's unbearable grief.
His mother, Maggie, was asked, "What would you say to the men
who shot your child?"

I expected to hear bitterness. Instead, her response was this:
"When they see what they have done, I hope they will turn away
from this kind of life."

These are the words of a friend, not an enemy. And that
was just the beginning. Maggie and Reg Green decided to offer an
extraordinary gift of friendship to the Italian people. They donated
Nicholas's organs to seven Italians, saving the lives of several of
them. His heart went to a Roman boy who had spent half his life in
the hospital. His liver went to a nineteen-year-old girl from Sicily
who was in her final coma. His kidneys went to a fourteen-year-old
girl and a ten-year-old boy whose lives had been completely ruled
by dialysis machines. Pancreas cells? They went to a woman in
Rome. Corneas? They went to two Sicilians. One was a woman who
had never seen her baby's face clearly. The other was a "rugby player
and a father of a young active family, whose world was gradually
darkening" (*The Nicholas Effect: A Boy's Gift to the World,* by Reg
Green, p. 23).

The Greens chose to be friends to the world, inspiring a
movement in which bank tellers donate kidneys to clients, and

strangers by the hundreds offer to be matched for bone marrow transplants. Viva Nicholas!

In this place of friendship, Tibetan monks show up in Detroit to make sand mandalas they later disperse into a deeply polluted river running through one the Western world's largest Arab communities. They tell us the mandala sand will help alleviate the pollution. When the monks leave, people are smiling, talking excitedly to complete strangers about the wonderful energy left behind by the Tibetans. Thinking about those monks, I suddenly realize that in every situation faced by an adventurer—and that is all of us—we have a choice. We can respond as friends, or not. Maybe this means giving someone a hug. Or saying, "I'm sorry," even though you weren't the reason a difficult situation surfaced. Maybe it is telling a coworker to get in the car because you're taking her to the psych ward at the local hospital before she tries to hurt herself again. Maybe it is taking the first step away from a tired old relationship dance that has harmed us for too long. In Buddha's time, friendship with the world meant that instead of destroying a country one of the kings had conquered after four horrific battles, he offered his daughter's hand to his young opponent. As family, they would no longer need to fight.

No more wars. In friendship this becomes possible.

eight

THE EIGHTH INGREDIENT:

Yoda's Wisdom

Size matters not. Look at me. Judge me by my size, do you? Hmmm?
Hmmm. And well you should not. For my ally is the Force, and a pow-
erful ally it is. Life creates it, makes it grow. Its energy surrounds us and
binds us. Luminous beings are we, not this crude matter. You must feel
the force around you; here, between you, me, the tree, the rock, every-
where, yes. Even between the land and the ship.

—Yoda

As crazy wisdom and a love adventure meld with the other
ingredients, real wisdom becomes the batter that bakes
into the chocolate cake of all of your lifetimes. But what is wisdom,
really? In five years I'll be sixty. Until recently that sounded really
old. Now it doesn't. Looking ahead to my red-haired, fishnet-
stocking days (assuming that I follow the footsteps of my beloved
great-grandmother), more than anything, I want to be wise.

For a long time Yoda was my wisdom model. He sees everything clearly and is a sage of few words. I've even dreamed about

him when I've been caught up in a stress-filled situation. The first time was in Chicago, about fifteen years ago. Babysitting a huge Zen Buddhist temple for my teacher over a weekend on short notice, as a beginning seminary student I had the unlucky job of delivering Sunday morning's formal sermon to what promised to be an auditorium's worth of really smart people. I figured that at least half of them were fully enlightened, which meant that the minute I opened my mouth they would see what a rookie I was and, of course, walk out.

To make matters worse, Phil Jackson (Phil Jackson!) lived in Chicago and was rumored to be Buddhist. Several of his staff had already found their way to the temple. I love Phil Jackson. I love the Chicago Bulls. I love Michael Jordan. It was possible that Phil would show up for my talk. Maybe he would bring Michael. Maybe they would bring me an autographed basketball. Maybe they would see how goofy I was—how wisdom free.

I was a mess.

I probably wrote out that sermon—a fifteen-minute dharma talk—twenty times. By Friday night I was having a hard time breathing, just thinking about it. By Saturday, hives had appeared on my calves.

Saturday night, when I finally fell asleep long past midnight, every dream was in Technicolor. In the one I most vividly remember I was in a desert, sitting under a palm tree, hoping someone would come rescue me. Looking up, I saw a figure walking slowly toward me, maybe a half mile away. As the figure got closer it looked like Muhammad. I knew him, by reputation, to be kind, so I was excited to see him. But just as I started to stand up to bow to him, he morphed into Jesus. All I could think was, "Oh, no, I've picked the wrong religion!" This thought became a loop in my brain as Jesus got closer and closer and it was replaced by, "I wonder if he'll hit me?" I still have no idea where that came from.

When Jesus got as close as, say, the end of a short driveway, he morphed into Yoda. Yoda with a slight smile.

Relieved, I sat back down. He came right up to me, still smiling his little Yoda smile. I figured he had shown up to dictate the dharma talk of the ages to me—one that Phil Jackson would like.

Suddenly we were nose to nose. He shouted, "Get over yourself!" and disappeared.

That was my introduction to big-*W* wisdom, wisdom that incorporates generosity, joy, ethics, spontaneity, adventure, and energy. He was telling me that all I needed to do was to unwrap myself from being so obsessed with the outcome and what people would think of me and just do my best. Instantly I could see how my need to look good, to sound more wise than I was, was making me crazy. And exhausted and, by then, sick.

Today I can't even remember the topic of Sunday's talk. I just did my best. Unfortunately, Phil didn't show.

Compassionate detachment is where Yoda was aiming me. Doing my best without being caught in outcomes. Doing my best when it may not solve the problem. Doing my best and then letting go when there clearly isn't anything else I can do. The world needs this wisdom. It is calmness in the face of the catastrophe we call life. It is calmness in the middle of the whole catastrophe, the one that always ends with death.

Calmness is a huge gift. And once you master it, you will be able to respond in a useful way to every difficult situation that decides to walk into your heart.

Here, for example, is a pretty typical Still Point day. By 6:30 a.m., one of the abbey residents is weeping hard. Her life is filled with heartbreaking situations right now. The pending death of her brother from leukemia at a too-young age. He will leave behind a wife and two young children. Difficult clients who want her to solve all the problems of their lives right now. An hour and a half later I get a phone call from a close friend. He has suddenly been fired. This man is a veritable Santa Claus to the children he counsels. He loves them beyond words, which is a good thing since he works with the toughest kids out there—the ones who defecate in their clothing at twelve or threaten foster parents with knives; the ones who have been ruined by cocaine-addicted mothers. The ones nobody wants.

The way the kids will find out that he is gone is when he simply doesn't show up for counseling sessions with them. He has no legal way to forewarn them of his absence. Once again they will know abandonment. For many of them his is the only love they know.

At 9:00 a.m., I stop to chat with the crossing guard at the front gate. I haven't seen her since last fall. She tells me there is a lockdown at the grade school a half block away. A student showed up with a knife. It was a third grader, she thinks. I tell her about my friend Keith's student—last week he was arrested for having an ounce of marijuana on school property. Seven policemen showed up. It was scary. The crossing guard tells me there are new drugs on the street this year. I groan. We just look at each other and sigh as she turns to greet a father who has walked over to say that the reason none of us has seen his daughter for a couple of weeks is because she is in a psychiatric hospital on Detroit's east side.

Then, for five hours, quiet, filled with manual work and letter writing. After which the melodramas start up again. Joe's truck breaks down on the highway. He and Andrea have to wait three and a half hours for a tow truck. When I turn on my e-mail, the messages are intense. A friend and her partner are being accused by their community of wrongdoings that are untrue. She wants to know how she can turn the tide of their anger. The last e-mail is from my dharma brother Mu Mun. On the previous night in Los Angeles he and his girlfriend were held up at gunpoint. So many people I love are in trouble.

Without some amount of compassionate detachment, I would be certifiably insane by the end of the day. Instead, at every turn, I am somehow able to stay planted in the middle of each situation—sometimes initially irritated or angry, mostly deeply saddened as each situation works its way through my system. I want to help, but how can I? What would Yoda do?

Just be calm, my heart replies. Just hear the story. I can do that. I can hear the story without raging at whatever machine seems to be creating the heartbreak—the truck manufacturer, the drug cabal, the social service system.

When I can stay calm, I'm amazed. The energy of the situation changes measurably. Smiles sprout. We can talk about next steps, possible solutions to seemingly intractable problems or how it is possible to stay fully present for a favorite brother who is dying young because that's what he needs more than anything else right now. This is what wisdom allows—a capacity for being completely present and helpful in one situation and then moving completely into the next situation that arises.

We aren't in charge of anyone else. The Buddha himself said, don't fix anyone else, just fix yourself:

> *Whoever would live well,*
> *Long lasting, bringing bliss—*
> *Let him be generous, be calm*
> *And cultivate the doing of good.*
> *By practicing these three...*
> *The wise one lives without regret*
> *His world infused with happiness.*

Without wisdom, this feels impossible. It is just so much easier to focus on a failing of someone or something else and then to go to town picking them apart. His mouth is always open when he eats. She never finishes a sentence without complaining about something. He is rude to waiters; she never says she is sorry. So we become nags, even if only in our minds. And we obsess. If only she would (fill in the blank). If only he would (fill in the blank). If I could add up all the days, weeks, years that I've spent focusing on how I could fix other people and trade that time in for simple prayer, I'd be so enlightened there wouldn't be any of me left. I'd be a series of clouds with smiley faces.

Wisdom tells us that we have our own work to do, each one of us. I can spend the rest of my life practicing not finishing other people's sentences for them and learning how to say, "I'm sorry," sooner. I can concentrate on the question "What can I do better?"

It has taken me a long time to realize how valuable these three things are in the face of a crisis. Especially calmness. Our ability to understand and affirm what is happening and still remain calm is desperately needed in a world rushing toward more caffeine, more speed, and mega-multitasking. Even when I am at a total loss about what to do to shift a situation, calm helps. I can feel it. And I can feel it when I give in to ranting and a friend's response is to smile and say something kind, like, "It is really hard, isn't it, Larkin?" They don't do my work for me, they just witness. And their calmness always gives me the space I need to see the next step clearly.

We become sages in the calmness. I'm convinced that this form of wisdom comes down to choice. Are we willing? If we say yes, in the words of the esteemed teacher Zalman Schachter-Shalomi, we are deciding to harvest our lives. Given that our life expectancies are now closing in on eighty-six for men and ninety-two for women (barring any meteor strikes, massive environmental disasters, war, or alien takeovers), we might as well give ourselves permission to be the "wise ones." We can demonstrate calmness and being present without getting sucked in to the vacuum cleaner of emotion that is always part of a crisis. We can out ourselves as intuitives. Simply admitting to myself that I might, in fact, be a wise person makes me wiser. When I am wiser, I'm able to look back at situations that completely sucked and from a longer view see how they helped me.

In the last article I wrote for Still Point's newsletter before moving on, I was asked, by me, about this: "What has been the hardest thing for you?"

Here is the response:

In our second year (at Still Point) Ananda Steve Bradley died. Although he was no longer a seminary student, I missed him enormously. Within a month of his death my root teacher, Samu Sunim, said some terribly untrue things about me in public. It took everything I had to stay put, to not run away. I had never had anyone so close to me really come after me before. I had heard Sunim say terrible things about other students who had left him but had always felt, somehow, that he wouldn't do that to me. I was wrong. In the end I'm grateful to him because he forced me to trust myself in the deepest way possible. In fact, when I confronted him about what he had done he told me that "Still Point will be stronger" for his actions. I now see that he was right.

Increased calmness, combined with clearheadedness, has also transformed me into a rabid conservationist and environmentalist. It happened suddenly, sort of like when my daughter was about eleven and one day, sitting next to me in the car, she changed before my very eyes. Gone was the Madonna-wanna-be I called "Sunshine." She had been taken over by an evil force and turned into a mouthy preteen who, in that moment, could not believe that she had the grave misfortune of getting the most stupid mother on the planet. It happened so fast, on a ride to swim practice, that on dropping her off I immediately went to three bookstores in Ann Arbor to find anything I could to explain the phenomenon. Happily, at the Borders on Liberty Street two strangers took pity on me and explained what had happened. She was a teenager. It would end someday. My daughter would be back. Their wisdom prevented me from buying a chocolate cake and eating the whole thing with my hands. Ten years later she was back and she liked me again.

A comparable transformation happened to me about six months ago. I woke up one morning and announced to myself that it is time to do everything I can to conserve the earth's resources. This means saying no to any livelihood that pays me more than I genuinely need for a simple lifestyle. It also means planting trees or buying trees to plant for everyone who asks me to share any celebration, from birthdays to bar mitzvahs. I have vowed to learn the local bus system by heart and, in three months, plan to spend thirty days without access to a car to see what else needs shifting. That I have a three-speed Schwinn with a basket on it for the grocery shopping will help. I've pledged to hold on to my old trusty Subaru for another 115,000 miles if it agrees. Recycling and regifting, always. I give books to the library and to friends and to friends of friends, and I already know the Seattle road I'll take on as the weekly volunteer trash gatherer.

The great surprise is how good this all feels. It is completely freeing to trade income in for manifesting wisdom in my own goofy way. And so far I haven't felt a need to be Madonna, but that could change.

The Frosting on the Cake: Access to Shared Wisdom

Wise people are desperately needed. Maybe an "Uncle Sam needs you" poster, only it would read, "The children of the world and their parents need *you*." They need mediators and watchdogs and rent-a-gramps for kids who have never met an old person. We can be quiet and listen. We can witness. We can give advice if asked. We can tell the truth.

My mother continues to be a role model here. These days she is teaching art at a senior center, partly, I'm certain, to help her students clearly see the problems facing our society right now—and how they can help. She's a black belt in computer-based communications; she knows where protests are and which prisoners could use some mail and what new policies are going to make us wonder, "What the hell were they thinking?" this time next year. There is no way she can possibly know what the outcome will be of all her hard work. Mom doesn't care.

Sages don't have anything to prove. They just help in whatever way they can.

In the Flower Ornament Sutra the character, Universal Good, watching us make a mess of our lives, finally raises his head in frustration and says he is going to explain something so we can all be happier.

"Wisdom is everywhere," he says.

Wisdom is everywhere. We can relax a little and watch for it, tap in to it. We can relax a little and be it.

Wisdom is everywhere. It is in the things we learn about ourselves even when we sit in front of our television sets. One of my biggest *ahas* ever was an episode of the television series *Sex and the City,* in which one of the main characters, Samantha, is fighting with a group of transvestites over who "owns" their street. Instead of escalating the scrapping, she throws a "kiss and make up" party. It works. I made peace with one of the toughest drug dealers in Detroit by taking him food. Two or three days a week I would watch him doing deals from our back window. In this neighborhood, calling the police doesn't change anything; they are overwhelmed as it is. The dealer ignored me until I offered him one of my nearly famous egg salad sandwiches on Avalon Bakery's organic wheat bread. While I wouldn't call us friends, he has stopped doing deals on his cell phone outside the back gate on our retreat days.

Oprah is walking, talking wisdom. So are many of her guests. The woman needs to run for president. If I started listing books that are wisdom incarnate, I'd never get anything else written for this chapter. So I won't. Okay, just one: Sue Monk Kidd's book—not one of the novels but the one about how she learned to trust herself, *The Dance of the Dissident Daughter*. It is a book laced with wisdom from beginning to end.

Admitting that each of us is wise energizes us to pay better attention to each other in the deepest way. The man standing next to you in the grocery line may be about to offer you the advice of a lifetime. Yesterday the man who runs the color printer at the copy shop gave me the best advice ever about getting through my next job hunt. "Don't worry," John told me. "Spend four months enjoying your life. Slow down. It is the best time ever. Then about three months before you really need to work, start looking. There will be something right there for you. God takes care of us." Wow. And I thought I was just there for twelve copies of a photograph.

In my last month at Still Point an old, old man shuffled past the abbey almost every afternoon, pushing a wheelchair. After every second step, he would stop to rest. If I'd crawled down the block my pace would have been faster. One afternoon I watched him for a few minutes from the doorway and then ran down the front steps to ask him if he would like me to push him for a couple of blocks. I glanced down at the seat of the chair and saw it was full of bags of candy he had just purchased at the Value dollar store on the other end of the block. When I asked him if he wanted help, he just grinned a huge toothless grin. "Oh, no, honey. This way the candy will be extra sweet."

Yoda is everywhere.

$\mathcal{B}$aking the $\mathcal{C}$ake

"Who was that Good Samaritan dude again?"
"He was the one who didn't walk past the freak spewing in the road.
I think it was in Egypt."

—Overheard porch conversation

When all the ingredients of the Chocolate Cake Sutra come together, they naturally feed each other and deepen. They merge into one delicious life. We naturally become more compassionate and kind. Our sense of humor deepens as we experience more and more of the world as just plain funny.

We become wise.

Like Gilgamesh, we discover that wisdom isn't an object to be grasped. And it can't be passed on. My mother can't make me wise as much as she wants to. I can't make you wise. You can't make anyone you love wise, either. In Zen we have a saying that a teacher can only point to the moon. It means that you and I have to do our own work. We have to have our own adventures. But when we do, wow.

Even when the path isn't clear, wow. In those times, which these days is all the time, all we can do is keep taking the next step. Author Stephen Mitchell offers a poignant quip about this truth: "When I argue with reality I lose, but only 100 percent of the time." Yes.

When we muster up the courage to stay on our path, rewards happen. We find joy. And we learn to fuel the transformation not by our egos but by living in reality, whatever it offers. We fuel the journey through our courage to question, our drive to find out who we really are underneath all our neurotic tendencies, and our growing compassion for everyone and everything that shares this space and time. Ultimately this journey leads us into a boundary-free zone, a place where we can be impartial, energy filled, irreverent, skeptical of moral absolutes, and, most of all, sane.

• • •

In this place, the law of karma becomes crystal clear. We see, often painfully, how one thing creates another. When I was a sophomore in college in New York City, I lived in a broken-down old building with a young Japanese woman, a tall, thin young woman from New Jersey, and an eighty-year-old woman who for reasons still unknown to me had permission to live in an apartment building owned by Columbia University.

We got along famously, the four of us. Except that Sarah, our tall, thin apartment mate, would stop eating for days at a time. Nothing except water. At the beginning of the school year she already looked too thin to me. By the end of October she was a stick figure with a head. By November the school had called her parents to say they needed to come get her. At the time I couldn't understand her inability to eat. She was beautiful. Smart. Funny. Interesting.

And dying.

The day her parents turned up, her whole eating karma unfolded in front of the rest of us. I was the one who answered the front door. With barely a nod, her father walked into the apartment, and the first words out of his mouth were "What's this mess?"

Here's the thing: the apartment was clean. I know clean, and it was clean. The four of us had spent a day scrubbing everything for her parents' visit, hoping it might make Sarah feel better. Once his mouth opened, her father never stopped finding fault. Nothing was right. The single dirty coffee cup in the sink shouldn't have been there. Why did we have a cat? Why were the dirty clothes hampers by the kitchen door instead of in the basement with the washing machine?

Her mother was worse. As soon as she saw the shape Sarah was in, *her* first words were "How could you do this to us?" I didn't hear the rest because I had to go hide in my room, overwhelmed by the sheer sadness of my apartment mate's situation. How could she not have stopped eating? As I suddenly saw it, she didn't have a chance.

You Decide

As our habits of generosity, energetic effort, radical ethics, tolerance, and clear seeing strengthen, we see that every single situation has its causes and that, in that moment, you and I can either help or hurt. When Koho was preparing for his ordination as a dharma teacher, he announced to the rest of us that he was going to do one hundred thousand prostrations—full bows to the ground—to get ready. He started out strong, maybe a thousand prostrations a week. But as we got closer to the ordination, other obligations meant that he wasn't going to make it.

The response was instant. Within a day a sign-up sheet appeared on the bulletin board, and people started signing up to do prostrations for him. Some of the names I didn't recognize. A few of us did thousands. It felt good.

Even after a few clearheaded choices, we trust ourselves more, relying on the Chocolate Cake Sutra's ingredients as vehicles for living a genuine, and genuinely happy, life. We don't need to guess. We simply need to pay attention. We don't even need to plan beyond a general sense of direction. When we pay attention, the path of our life becomes obvious, sometimes painfully so. (Consider yourself warned.)

Accepting what is leads to the surprise of a lifetime. Suddenly you realize that happiness is yours. And that it grows from the opposite of what you expect. Instead of control, it grows from letting go. Instead of stuff, it grows from simplicity. Instead of the need for fifteen minutes of fame, it grows from planting flowers and vegetables in an abandoned city plot—anonymously.

My mouth still gets me into trouble sometimes. Most recently it was during a winter walk with a friend of mine. She was complaining about her life, mostly small stuff—a broken dryer, a sloppy partner, the long winter. At one point she literally stopped in the middle of the trail and looked at me.

"I don't think I can ever be happy."

Without thinking, I looked at her and said, "Oh, that's just because you don't want to be."

In an instant, one less friend. She didn't talk to me all the way back to the car, didn't talk to me in the car, hasn't talked to me since.

I miss her, which has led me to think a lot about happiness. I've realized that although what I said was unskillful, it was true. Happiness can happen only when we let it. When we choose it. I see choosing it as a moral obligation, at least for those of us who want the world to be a better place for everyone. It's separate from the people in our lives or the situations we find ourselves in. In fact, finding happiness in the day-to-day life we've been given is surprisingly, embarrassingly, simple. Why? Because it is available the instant we allow our senses to take in the surroundings, the views, the moments, smells, and tastes that we completely miss out on when we are too busy listing all the reasons why we aren't happy.

Maybe I'm missing something here, but every teaching I've read from spiritual teachers big and small has implied the possibility of happiness. Buddha was pretty adamant about it. "Live in peace. Live in joy." We have the ingredients. They meld together in the land of "just this." And while it is true that I continue to wait for a scientific breakthrough that through the miracle of drugs will make me two

inches taller (and therefore lithe), I've learned that accepting what
is gives me two gifts. The first is the mental room to actually notice
what is happening. The second is a growing appreciation for all of it.
My shortness doesn't prevent me from sighing over the purple-blue of
night backing the statue of Tara when I do early morning prayers in
my room. The sweetness of morning chants, the smell of coffee brew-
ing, the sheer cuddliness of my meditation cushion—none of these
depends on anything going on in my life externally, not the loss of a
good friend, the demands of a tough job, the cold of a child. And these
are just the wonders that hit before 7:00 a.m. It is amazing that any of
us can make it through a day with all the sights, sounds, smells, and
textures lying in wait to thrill and entertain.

Here's another confession related to clear seeing: Every time
I've chosen the complicated route, when the choice was between
that and a simple one, it has made me miserable. A camera I don't
understand. Anything but a user-friendly computer. A foreign
car. A murky relationship where the ground rules aren't clear. By
contrast, when I've gone the simple route, it has always brought me
great happiness. A point-and-shoot camera. A Mac. The iPod. A car
with pictures for instructions in the owner's manual. Someone who
just plain loves me, chanting and all.

The Te of Piglet by Benjamin Hoff offers a terrific teaching
on how readily available happiness is, all the time. In the words of
Taoist alchemist and herbalist Ko Hung: "The contented man can

be happy with what appears to be useless." He can, he can. And in the middle of all of it, joy. And that is just the beginning, or as T. S. Eliot put it:

> *I said to my soul be still,*
> *and wait without hope*
> *Wait without thought ...*
> *So the darkness shall be the light,*
> *and the stillness the dancing.*

$\mathcal{A}$ $\mathcal{S}weet$ $\mathcal{L}ife$

Things not to worry about:
    Don't worry about popular opinion . . .
    Don't worry about the past
    Don't worry about the future
    Don't worry about growing up
    Don't worry about anybody getting ahead of you
    Don't worry about triumph
    Don't worry about failures . . .
    Don't worry about mosquitoes
    Don't worry about flies
    Don't worry about insects in general
    Don't worry about parents . . .
    Don't worry about disappointments
    Don't worry about pleasures
    Don't worry about satisfactions

                    —F. Scott Fitzgerald

If I didn't start painting I would have raised chickens.

                    —Grandma Moses

*I*n book 7 of the Flower Ornament Sutra, Shakyamuni Buddha has just attained true awakening. Word is out that there is a holy man, and characters show up in droves to hear his teachings. It's like a Bruce Springsteen or White Stripes concert, only bigger. They all hope that he will reveal to them "the great Buddha fields, the great awakening." And he does, but not exactly in the way they expect. He appears to each character as the specific teacher each one needs.

Manjushri, one of the most famous bodhisattvas in the Buddhist bodhisattva collective, watches this happen and just can't keep quiet about it. He has to explain: "All the Buddhas in the worlds in ten directions know that the inclinations of sentient beings are not the same and so they teach and train them according to their needs and capacities!" Everywhere, everywhere, there are teachers trying to get us to understand the value of generosity and clarity and ethics and the rest of the behaviors I have been writing about, by now almost ad nauseam, yes?

So when we ask ourselves, Is the teacher our child? Our pet? Our nosy neighbor? Our partner? Our boss? Our president? the answer is yes. Everyone is our teacher, doing his or her utmost best to help us get to the land of rejoicing. Maybe she is teaching us heedfulness. I think of my extremely organized younger sister who, even when we were in grade school, set out her entire uniform the night before school so she could put it on in about three minutes while the rest of us ran around like chickens with our heads cut off trying to piece enough of our uniforms together to get through the day without too many demerits.

Maybe he is teaching us acceptance, or at least to stop picking which moments we're going to enjoy. When I drove out to Providence, Rhode Island, a few years ago to check out the Rhode Island School of Design, the bed-and-breakfast I stayed in was pretty wild. First, there were no lights anywhere, even inside, and I arrived at night. Not good. But my room, when I found it, was adorable. Good. But then, its towels were dirty. Not good. But the bed was comfy. Good. The entire stay was a parade of good, not-good moments until, out of sheer exhaustion, I just stopped thinking them. The owner couldn't have done a better job of forcing me to see my own parade of mental states.

Who is my teacher, the person or thing pointing me in the direction of behaviors that will open up happiness? I think of Issa, who becomes completely enraptured each time his mother breast-feeds him. Or Amy, who was a dervish of energy when she decided to clean the entire abbey, top to bottom, in a day. The ducks on the river in Providence never changed their pace or direction during the afternoon I watched them, even though at least three weather fronts hit—rain, snow, sleet. No matter. Tranquillity.

Who is my teacher? The fellow who ran the bed-and-breakfast in Providence tried hard to give me a decent breakfast even though it was clear that even the most simple chores were difficult for him. When he dropped the bagels off the serving plate and they went flying up like a cloud and then fell all over the dining room, he simply started all over again with a new plate of bagels. He refused to stop trying to bring in a full plate of baked goods even though it took more than four tries. His concentration was palpable.

I stop in a Providence café in the middle of the afternoon. A young woman comes in with her grandmother. The grandmother sits down at a small table by the window while the young woman goes up to the counter to ream into the owner about all the things wrong with the sandwiches he had delivered to them. At first the man is funny and teases her. But when she doesn't back down he argues hard with her, refusing to give her any money back since she has eaten the food. Through all of this, the grandmother sits quietly, with a small smile on her face, not missing a thing. She just waits for the two of them to calm down, which they do, eventually making peace over a new sandwich, which they split with a Dr. Brown's Cream Soda. I feel like I've just watched two-thirds of a great opera, except nobody dies and we all leave smiling.

Always Rejoice

Two chapters later in the Flower Ornament Sutra, Buddha is throwing out truths to the crowd right and left. So much energy is generated by his effort that the characters surrounding him once again can't keep their mouths shut. So they also start shouting teachings right and left. It is hilarious. They are just too happy to sit still.

Then a wonderful sentence appears: "Always rejoicing, they go to all lands to explain such a teaching for all."

When I first read the sentence it stopped me in my tracks. Always rejoicing. Not sometimes rejoicing or occasionally rejoicing. Always.

Rejoicing is about being glad or happy. When I visited China in my thirties I was surprised, I am embarrassed to admit, by how happy people were. I don't know exactly what I thought I would see, but having read novels and history books about the cruelties of the various regimes, I didn't expect to hear laughter. Yet people laughed often. I didn't expect to see smiles, but grins were everywhere.

Finally, well into the trip, I asked a young tour guide about it. We were standing outside the front door of a temple. He pointed to a sign over the entrance. "It says, Ten thousand joys, ten thousand sorrows." While it was true that the Chinese people had their share of sorrows, they also had an equal amount of joy in their lives. After our conversation I saw the sign everywhere. Joys and sorrows. Many of both.

In our society we've got the sorrows part down. We are skilled at being sad, pissed, depressed, angry, and filled with despair. I see these on a daily basis. What I don't see as much are belly chortles, grins, smiles, laughter. Somehow, even when the news is good, even when a situation is infused with beauty, we seem to have forgotten how to rejoice.

Thank goodness for the Issas, the ducks, and the Italian grandmothers. They remind us that while life is about sorrow, it is also about joy. I think of my granddaughter, Patty. When I went to Portland, Oregon, to teach a seminar on building a business for

the Dharma Rain sangha, she was three. Patty lives near Portland.
About twenty minutes before the end of the class, I saw a movement
out of the corner of my eye. Suddenly this little kid came racing
straight at me, leaped onto me, and Velcroed herself to my hip. She
was so thrilled to see me (as I was to see her!) that she wouldn't get
down, wouldn't stop laughing and hugging. She was filled with joy,
and her joy made the rest of us laugh and fill up with wide-grin
happiness. A rejoice teacher was in our midst.

My friends Sansae and Sanho have a tiny dog that cannot
believe his good luck when you walk into their house. Every time I
visit, he literally jumps a couple of feet straight up, runs around me
like there was no tomorrow, and does back flips because he just can't
keep his happiness inside. We always laugh. Another rejoice teacher.

Or at his ordination, Kogam was so happy that he literally
picked me up off the ground in a bear hug. I am fairly confidant
that his action was a first for a formal ordination. The whole room
laughed with him. We were, in that moment, a community rejoicing.

The sign over the Chinese temple didn't say ten thousand
sorrows, six hundred joys. Or ten thousand sorrows, one thousand
joys. We get both. We get to rejoice. It is good to practice before
we forget what it feels like to be genuinely happy, to see and taste
and hear all the reasons to rejoice. The ones that are doing their
best to stare us down as I write, even smack in the middle of tough
times. As long as people populate the earth there will always be an
Iraq. Sorrow, sorrow, sorrow. And there will always be puppies and

babies being born and sunflowers and delicious chocolate cake. Joy, joy, joy.

• • •

Sitting with a new friend in a café that has quickly become a favorite hangout. It's the cupcakes. They bake hundreds every day, and you can watch one of the baristas frost them while you wait for coffee. It is impossible to walk away from the counter cake free. I already have to limit myself to one visit a week. Even the smell of the place turns my brain to mush.

My friend has just asked me about this book. I tell him that it is about how everyone and everything is precious. A pause. Everyone is holy. He leans into the table to listen closely, without saying anything. So far, so good. Then he asks about the behaviors. I go over them one by one: giving joy, ethical behavior, tolerance, the capacity to keep going, clearheadedness, crazy wisdom, being adventurous. I tell him that I didn't come up with them, that they come from an old sutra, the Flower Ornament Sutra, which is over twelve hundred years old. He says they make sense as I describe them, that he has always tried to be generous and tolerant and clearheaded. I already know that he tries to be open to new people, places, and things. Otherwise he would never be sitting here for the better part of a morning with someone so new to the city. As a master carpenter, he spends a lot of hours working with the apprentices on his project, training them to pay attention to what they are doing.

I'm surprised by his reaction. He isn't a Buddhist. Actually he isn't anything, at least formally.

"You know," he says, grinning, "I've always suspected that everyone is holy. I've just never heard anyone say it out loud like this before. And actually mean it. This calls for a cupcake."

Ah, Seattle, sweet, sweet Seattle.

May all beings be free.

February 14, 2006

Barbara Downing's Perfect Chocolate Cake*

INGREDIENTS:

6 Tablespoons baking cocoa

1 cup white sugar

4 eggs

1⅔ cups self-rising flour

a pinch of salt

8 oz. (2 sticks) butter

Preheat oven to 350°F. Grease two eight-inch layer cake pans (or anything that comes close). Cream the butter and sugar together. Add the salt and well-beaten eggs. Then add the cocoa and flour (through a sieve if you have one) to the butter mixture. Try not to eat it.

Pour the cake batter into the pans, and bake them for 20 to 25 minutes or until a toothpick inserted in the center comes out clean. Don't overcook.

Frosting isn't necessary with this cake. But if you insist: just melt a stick or so of butter, add as much powdered sugar as it takes to look like frosting, dropping in a couple of teaspoons of milk if you overdo the sugar. Also add at least 1 teaspoon of real vanilla to the sugar-butter-milk mixture. You'll have to wait for the cake to cool before you frost it. Good luck. I've never been able to wait that long.

This cake is best eaten immediately with three friends. Each person gets a spoon and something to drink and digs in.

*Any cake eaten in pure awareness—without the distractions of a cell phone, computer, television, or conversation—is a perfect chocolate cake. This includes cakes that have been in your freezer since last February. I know this.